I0191797

I wholeheartedly recommend this sacred resource to anyone who is walking the road of caregiving and wondering if they can keep going. Julie reminds us that we don't do this in our strength. We do it with God's sustaining grace.

—*Pat Layton*
Author, *Life Unstuck: Finding Peace with Your Past, Purpose in Your Present, Passion for Your Future* and *Surrendering the Secret: Healing the Heartbreak of Abortion*

Endorsements for *Overflowing Grace: Finding Strength to Carry on as a Caregiver* by Julie K. Gillies:

A lifeline for weary caregivers! *Overflowing Grace* offers biblical hope and practical wisdom for those walking the sacred yet exhausting path of caring for loved ones. Julie graciously reminds you that God sees every sacrifice you make.

—Rachel Wojo
Author, *Desperate Prayers*
Caregiver for twenty-two years

The most vital key for not just surviving but thriving your season of caregiving is to stay close to Jesus. My husband, Bill, and I just completed a ten-year assignment of caregiving to his elderly parents. What surprised us was the past three years: I was plunged into a coma, then, as I recovered, I was diagnosed with ovarian cancer! Bill was caregiving for his folks *and* me. That is *exactly why* caregivers need wise, empathetic, and biblical encouragement, such as is found in this book by Julie Gillies. You just never know what might be next! This book is a *lifeline* of *hope*!

—Pam and Bill Farrel
Best-selling authors of over sixty books, including *Men Are Like Waffles, Women Are Like Spaghetti*; and Pam's coauthored *Discovering Hope in the Psalms: A Creative Bible Study Experience*
Co-Directors, Love-Wise Ministries

Having a father who was diagnosed with Alzheimer's disease at fifty-six years of age, I understand the weary weightiness of being a caregiver...and so does Julie Gillies. With honesty and vulnerability, she becomes a friend who understands what you're going through. These short devotions are like a warm hug from God when you need it most. I highly recommend *Overflowing Grace* and wish I'd had it years ago.

—Sharon Jaynes
Author of twenty-six books, including *When You Don't Like Your Story: What If Your Worst Chapters Could Become Your Greatest Victories?* and *The Power of a Woman's Words: How the Words You Say Shape the Lives of Others*

If you're a caregiver or know someone who needs strength and encouragement on their caregiving journey, *Overflowing Grace* can help. Having been in the trenches herself, Julie Gillies speaks into the lives of other caregivers with reassuring, Scripture-infused words that empathize, uplift, and give needed insight. As a caregiver myself, I found Julie's prayers to be a balm for my weary heart as I made them my own. Julie points caregivers to the Lord, where they'll find the unfailing strength they need.

—*Cheryl Barker*
Author, *Christmas for the Heart: 25 Devotions Reclaiming the Beauty and Wonder of the Season*

Caregiving is overwhelming and exhausting, and it often pushes us to our limit. It's also a blessing, a gift, and an opportunity to give something precious to someone we love dearly. Caregiving, however, makes it easy to lose ourselves. Julie Gillies understands this, and the words on these pages will fill your soul, giving you what you need to continue caregiving.

—*Jill Savage*
Host, *No More Perfect Podcast*
Author, *199 Prayers for Your Husband*

As someone who walks alongside women navigating life's unexpected assignments, I find Julie's book to be a lifeline of grace and truth. *Overflowing Grace* is not just a message—it's a ministry to the weary-hearted caregiver. With raw honesty, deep biblical wisdom, and her signature comforting voice, Julie invites us into her caregiving journey and gently leads us to the feet of Jesus, where strength is renewed and purpose is rediscovered.

This book is a much-needed reminder that our current place—though painful and often stretching—is not outside God's plan. Whether you're caring for a parent, spouse, child, or grandchild, this is a guidebook for the soul that whispers, "You are seen. You are chosen. You are not alone."

A 60-DAY DEVOTIONAL

Overflowing GRACE

FINDING STRENGTH TO CARRY ON AS A CAREGIVER

JULIE K. GILLIES

WHITAKER
HOUSE

Unless otherwise noted, all Scripture quotations are taken from the *Christian Standard Bible*®, Copyright © 2017 by Holman Bible Publishers. Used by permission. Christian Standard Bible® and CSB® are federally registered trademarks of Holman Bible Publishers. Scripture quotations marked (AMPC) are taken from the *Amplified® Bible* (AMPC), Copyright © 1954, 1958, 1962, 1964, 1965, 1987 by The Lockman Foundation. Used by permission. Lockman.org. Scripture quotations marked (NLT) are taken from the *Holy Bible, New Living Translation*, copyright ©1996, 2004, 2015 by Tyndale House Foundation. Used by permission of Tyndale House Publishers, Carol Stream, Illinois 60188. All rights reserved. Scripture quotations marked (ESV) are taken from *The ESV® Bible* (The Holy Bible, English Standard Version®), © 2001 by Crossway, a publishing ministry of Good News Publishers. Used by permission. All rights reserved.

OVERFLOWING GRACE
Finding Strength to Carry on as a Caregiver (A 60-Day Devotional)

Julie K. Gillies
www.JulieGillies.com

ISBN: 979-8-88769-451-1
eBook ISBN: 979-8-88769-452-8
Printed in the United States of America
© 2025 by Julie Gillies

Whitaker House
1030 Hunt Valley Circle
New Kensington, PA 15068
www.whitakerhouse.com

Library of Congress Control Number: 2025903825

No part of this book may be reproduced or transmitted in any form or by any means, electronic or mechanical—including photocopying, recording, or by any information storage and retrieval system—without permission in writing from the publisher. Please direct your inquiries to permissionseditor@whitakerhouse.com.

1 2 3 4 5 6 7 8 9 10 11 〓 32 31 30 29 28 27 26 25

INTRODUCTION

Becoming a caregiver has impacted, interrupted, and altered my life. I have cried, prayed, resented, and then wrestled with guilt for feeling resentful, then repented. I have grappled with anger, forgiven, let go of expectations, loved till it hurt, and, in a miraculous flow of God's effusive grace, been able to (finally) make peace with my lot. I have even managed to find joy and satisfaction in a season I neither anticipated nor wanted.

If you are reading this book, you may feel similarly. You may have recently become a caregiver as well. Or perhaps you've been caring for a loved one long-term. Whatever your current caregiving situation, you are far from alone. According to the Family Caregiver Alliance, approximately 43.5 million caregivers have provided unpaid care to an adult or child in the last twelve months.[1]

Perhaps you are caring for an aging parent. Maybe you are acting as a caregiver to your spouse. Possibly, you're taking long-term care of a disabled child. Or perhaps, like me, you are caring for a grandchild. As believers, we realize that God sometimes brings challenging assignments into our lives at various times. This doesn't always mean we're prepared for or feel up to the challenge. Nor does it mean we're happy about it, at least not initially. But what I've come to understand over the last four-plus years of caring for our precious (and exhausting) granddaughter is that to be successful—and to retain our sanity in this season—three things must happen.

First, we must accept our current reality. No denial here. No ignoring the truth. This means that we recognize our help is now absolutely required and that our lives are likely to look different than the way we thought they would, at least for now. It means that we don't fight, argue, and fall into self-pity (or at least that we don't stay

---

1. "Caregiver Statistics: Demographics," Family Caregiver Alliance, accessed September 11, 2024, https://www.caregiver.org/resource/caregiver-statistics-demographics/.

there). Accepting our lot means being willing to face reality and do our part, whatever is required of us. And the kicker? As believers, we have to do it all with a good attitude, not as whiny, complaining grumps.

Second, we must surrender to our current reality. Surrender is an inner stance. It's a heart issue, one that requires submission to the God who allowed our situation to happen. It's a humble place of accepting God's sovereignty and the position He has placed us in. And, yes, He has indeed placed us here. Psalm 31:15 assures us, *"The course of my life is in your power."* Though we don't always understand our paths, it's reassuring to know that God truly directs the course of our lives. Yes, even here and now, while we care for our loved ones. When we acknowledge God's sovereignty, knowing that He is kind, good, and faithful, and will surely help us, we can more easily choose to surrender to even this difficult challenge. Our authentic surrender ushers in God's grace because, according to James 4:6, *"God resists the proud but gives grace to the humble."*

Third, we must remember that we cannot meet our current care-giving challenge in our own strength. It's simply not humanly possible. The good news is that God, who is at work in our hearts and lives, actually provides us with the power to accomplish our hardest tasks. Once we accept our position and surrender to Him, He changes our desires, giving us grace to willingly lay down our lives in this season. It's all for God's good pleasure, satisfaction, and delight. Did you catch that? We're not only helping our loved one, but we're also honoring God as we work, bringing Him pleasure, satisfaction, and delight. (See Philippians 2:13, below.) Imagine bringing almighty God—the Maker of the universe and of you—pleasure and delight!

As you embark on or continue in this caregiving season, my prayer for you is that when faced with your inadequacies and short-comings (trust me, this happens daily), you won't just crumble but will remember to cry out for *His* strength. That's what this book is all about—crying out to almighty God to provide the strength and daily grace we need for this caregiving season. God is absolutely faithful. He will never fail to provide the grace and strength we need.

> *[Not in your strength] for it is God Who is all the while effectually at work in you [energizing and creating in you the power and desire], both to will and to work for His good pleasure and satisfaction and delight.*   —(Philippians 2:13 AMPC)

YOU ARE WHERE YOU'RE SUPPOSED TO BE

A person's steps are established by the LORD.
—Psalm 37:23

If, since beginning your caregiving assignment, you have at some point struggled with it all—the situation itself, the timing, and the many implications for your life personally—I understand. Grappling with what I call caregiving side effects (uncertainty, confusion, disappointment, and grief, to name a few) is our natural human response to the changes and all of the new demands we face.

But if today's verse is true—and it definitely is—then this changes everything. It should change our perspective. It should change how we view our current, God-given assignment. And, ultimately, it should ease our souls.

Whether you feel you had a choice in your current circumstances or not is irrelevant. God chose you—He has chosen every one of us to step up and step in. I find this truth reassuring. We aren't subject to the whims of fate. We aren't compelled by anyone else's decisions. We don't need to rely solely on ourselves to determine if we're in the right place. Because we believe that God has ordered our steps, we can trust that we are exactly where we're supposed to be. This means God Himself orchestrated each one of us to be at this precise place and time on our current caregiving journey.

Since God has orchestrated our being here, in this caregiving place, our choices are simple. We can resent it, or we can embrace it. If we are wise, we will not give in to resentment, which poisons our souls and harms those around us. Instead, we can choose to continually surrender to the season God has allowed, embracing His current plans and purposes for us. We can, like Jesus, pray, *"Nevertheless, not my will, but yours, be done"* (Luke 22:42)…and mean it.

As we trust that God has established our steps and placed us here, we can, by God's grace, experience deep soul satisfaction and true soul peace, knowing we're precisely where we're supposed to be, doing the exact work He requires of us for now.

A CAREGIVER PRAYER

Lord, You know the degree to which I have struggled as a caregiver. Right now, I choose to trust that You have placed me here, in this current place and time, by design. Will You please help me to change my perspective, change how I view this assignment, and ease my soul as I surrender to and embrace this place?

Help me not to give in to resentment. Where that has happened, please forgive me and grant me a willing heart to sustain me. Whatever my desires or hopes may be, nevertheless, not my will, but Your will, be done. I surrender to this assignment and choose by Your great grace to embrace it. Strengthen and help me every step of the way. In Jesus's name, amen.

THOUGHTS FOR TODAY

+ My steps are established by God.

+ God has orchestrated for me to be here at this precise place and time.

+ I can surrender to and embrace this season and have true soul peace.

MY THOUGHTS AND PRAYERS

_____

_____

_____

_____

_____

_____

DAY TWO
IMPERFECT CAREGIVERS UNITE

*O Lord, you are so good, so ready to forgive, so full of unfailing
love for all who ask for your help.*
—Psalm 86:5 NLT

Not one of us is capable of being the perfect caregiver. We drop the ball. We forget what we ought to remember. We grow weary and discouraged. We lose our temper. We are frail people caring for frail people, and although we make a gargantuan effort, the reality is that we will occasionally fail. Our response to our failure(s) matters and makes all the difference.

One of my typical responses when faced with my failure is stabbing myself with a harpoon of guilt. "How could I? Why didn't I just…? What is my problem?" But James reminds us that *"we all stumble in many ways. If anyone does not stumble in what he says, he is mature, able also to control the whole body"* (James 3:2). We *all* stumble. We all blow it. To be honest, our failures shouldn't come as a surprise. Not one of us can control everything we say and do. It's not humanly possible. There's an odd comfort in knowing we are not alone in our shortcomings—even better, in knowing that we have a good and faithful God who is ready to forgive.

When our imperfections jump up and smack us in the face, there's no point in denying the truth, and there's no point in dragging out our harpoons. Our heavenly Father is so kind; He is so good and so ready to forgive! Just meditate on that for a moment. Almighty God is not reluctant to forgive. He's not pointing a condemning finger at us. He stands, arms open, ready to forgive His confessing child. All we have to do is run to Him and say, "Oh, Lord, please forgive me!" And because we know and trust in Jesus, that's exactly what He does.

When we're baffled and grieved by our shortcomings and failures, how remarkable and wonderful it is to know that the Lord is bursting with unfailing love for all who ask His help. He doesn't resent our asking for help; He stands ready to assist us. Jesus knows that apart from Him, we can do nothing (see John 15:5), so He enables us to pick ourselves up, brush ourselves off, and jump back into the tasks at hand. His unfailing love reinstates us, fills us, and equips us, His imperfect caregivers, to serve our loved ones with energy and joy.

A CAREGIVER'S PRAYER

Lord, I admit that I simply am not capable of being a perfect caregiver, and I will fail at times. Will You please help me not to stab myself with a harpoon of guilt but instead run to You, my faithful God, because You stand ready to forgive me when I blow it? Thank You, Lord, that You are not reluctant to forgive me, but You stand, arms open, ready to forgive me, Your confessing child.

Help me remember to ask for Your help. Thank You that when I do, Your unfailing love rushes in, pouring grace into me and enabling me to do what I clearly cannot do apart from You, Jesus. Cleanse me, reinstate me, and enable me to serve my loved one with great energy and joy. In Jesus's name, amen.

THOUGHTS FOR TODAY

+ There's a comfort in knowing I am not alone in my shortcomings and failures.

+ Almighty God is not reluctant to forgive me. He's not pointing a condemning finger at me but stands, arms open, ready to forgive me, His confessing child.

+ When I'm baffled and grieved by my failures, how wonderful it is to know that the Lord is bursting with unfailing love for all who ask for His help.

MY THOUGHTS AND PRAYERS

_____

_____

_____

_____

_____

_____

DAY THREE
HIS STRENGTH IS BETTER

He gives power to the weak and strength to the powerless.
—Isaiah 40:29 NLT

I sometimes wonder if God chuckles sympathetically as He watches His children struggle under heavy loads He never intended for them to carry, not unlike an adult watching a young child struggling to carry his dad's big boots across the living room. It's sort of cute and comical. The adult knows that the child can't possibly lift and carry those big old boots, but the toddler hasn't figured it out yet, and so they grunt and try. Hard. Soon enough, though, wailing tears of frustration signal their surrender. That's when, as parents or grandparents, we step in, pick up the boots, and help our precious babies carry them to the back door.

How many times do we, as caregivers, act the same way as the toddler in this illustration? We see a task that needs to be accomplished, and off we go in our strength, straining and grunting, without a thought or prayer for assistance from the One whose help we absolutely require.

If, as Jesus said, *"Apart from me you can do nothing"* (John 15:5 NLT), why do we forge ahead, attempting to help our loved one in our own feeble power? Are we as clueless as toddlers? Is it simply that we don't understand our human limitations? Or could human pride be to blame?

As caregivers, we are attempting to assist in situations that may involve a crisis, a long-term health issue, or hospice care. All sad. All hard. All beyond our human capacity to adequately manage and handle, apart from Christ.

The Lord delights in our prayers. (See Proverbs 15:8.) So why do we hesitate to ask Him for strength, wisdom, grace, and help? Especially when the load is so heavy? Our loving heavenly Father simply waits for us to ask. Perhaps, just as we would watch a determined toddler figure out that they need our help with heavy lifting, He waits for us to admit defeat so He can carry the boots to the back door.

In seasons when we are weary and entirely out of our league, how awesome it is to know that we serve the everlasting God who *never* grows weak or weary. (See Isaiah 40:28.) May He give us, His caregiver servants, the wisdom and grace to ask for what we clearly don't have, and what He clearly offers to His struggling children. May our hearts rejoice in deep gratitude that He really does give power to the weak and strength to the powerless.

A CAREGIVER PRAYER

Lord, forgive me for all the times I attempt to do things in my own strength. Help me remember that You truly delight in my prayers and that You are simply waiting for me to ask for help. So, Lord, I am asking for help now. My strength is limited, and my power evaporates long before the day's tasks are over. Will You please strengthen my weary body and give me grace to serve my loved one well, for Your glory?

There are days I feel so out of my league, but, God, I am grateful that You never grow weak or weary and for the strength and power You provide. Help me remember that apart from You, I can do nothing. Please remain close to me and help me cling to You, and I will do my best to honor You in this caregiving journey. In the precious name of Jesus, amen.

THOUGHTS FOR TODAY

+ I don't have to face this season in my own power.

+ Apart from Christ, I cannot manage well, so I will ask for His help.

+ I will rejoice that God provides power and strength for each task.

MY THOUGHTS AND PRAYERS

_____

_____

_____

_____

_____

_____

DAY FOUR
A HOLY CALLING

Teach me to do your will, for you are my God. May your
gracious Spirit lead me on level ground.
—Psalm 143:10

If you've ever hiked on steep, rocky terrain, you understand that each step is arduous. Foot placement is crucial, and caution rules the day as one attempts to navigate loose dirt and precariously positioned rocks on an ever-escalating path. Even a walk in hilly woods can be cause for caution, with tree roots, holes, stones, and tall grasses where poison ivy or snakes may lurk. Awareness of one's surroundings is imperative. Exhaustion is certain.

Such is the caregiver's season. This holy calling, fraught with steep hills of doubt and frustration, can be an emotionally winding road filled with potential tripping hazards, such as uncertainty, fear, and exhaustion. There's always the risk of falling into hopelessness or despair.

Thank God we don't walk through it all for no purpose. In the psalm above, while being pursued by his enemies, David appeals to the Lord for instruction. He asks God to teach him to do His will. It's a desperate but wise request. If we are wise, we will do the same.

What does the Lord teach us as we hike our caregiving journey?

+ He teaches us to rely on and trust Him: *"God arms me with strength, and he makes my way perfect"* (Psalm 18:32 NLT).

+ He teaches us the meaning of true servanthood: *"[Jesus] poured water into a basin and began to wash his disciples' feet and to dry them with the towel tied around him"* (John 13:5).

+ He teaches us humility: *"[Jesus] gave up his divine privileges; he took the humble position of a slave and was born as a human being"* (Philippians 2:7 NLT).

+ He teaches us to surrender and say what Jesus said: *"Father, if you are willing, take this cup away from me—nevertheless, not my will, but yours, be done"* (Luke 22:42).

+ He teaches us to persevere: *"But as for you, brothers and sisters, do not grow weary in doing good"* (2 Thessalonians 3:13).

As we serve in the caregiver capacity, which is a holy calling, we are emulating Christ, becoming more like Jesus in the process. And as we pray and trust Him to help us daily—sometimes minute by minute—in His great faithfulness, the Lord guides us, leading us out of the pitfalls of hopelessness and despair and onto the level ground of spiritual growth, maturity, and a deeper trust in and reliance on Him.

A CAREGIVER PRAYER

Lord, thank You that I am not hiking through this difficult caregiving journey for no reason. Thank You that there is a purpose in all of this and that, when I feel desperate, I can do more than ask for help. I can ask You to teach me. Lord, teach me how to rely on and trust You more. Teach me humility and how to be a faithful servant in this season. Give me the grace to surrender my expectations and desires and to persevere when the hike is steep, rugged, and difficult.

Lead me out of the treacherous paths of discouragement and despair. Encourage my sometimes-uncertain heart and fill it with hope and courage as I learn to trust You and rely on You more. Lord, help me and make me more like Jesus as I walk out this holy calling. It's in His name that I pray. Amen.

THOUGHTS FOR TODAY

+ I don't walk through these hard days for no purpose.

+ God is teaching me through this process.

+ My caregiving journey is a holy calling.

MY THOUGHTS AND PRAYERS

FLOURISHING WHERE YOU'RE PLANTED

I am like a flourishing olive tree in the house of God; I trust in God's faithful love forever and ever.
—Psalm 52:8

Is it possible to flourish emotionally, spiritually, and even physically while we're caregivers? The answer is a resounding yes! I have discovered four absolutely vital disciplines that have helped me thrive in my role as a caregiver.

First, we flourish by sharing our concerns, and regularly praying, with a trusted loved one. Don't allow yourself to become or remain isolated. You don't have to disclose details or betray any privacy issues, but it seriously lightens the load to talk with someone trustworthy who cares and will pray with you. We desperately need prayer support at this critical time!

Second, we flourish by planting ourselves in the house of God. Don't neglect your spiritual health. Attend church as often as you can. Make time to read God's Word daily. This vital habit provides spiritual sustenance we genuinely require as caregivers. When my daughter was a newborn, she rarely slept and cried nonstop. Seriously sleep-deprived, I could scarcely function, let alone sit down and read a chapter of the Bible. So, I read just one sentence each night before collapsing onto my pillow. I'm convinced that my desire to make space and time for Scripture honored God, and He used that small amount of truth to sustain me.

Third, we flourish when we care for ourselves physically. Caregiving requires strong, healthy bodies. So, we need to do our part to the best of our abilities. I am a huge proponent of taking daily walks outdoors. Feeling the wind, hearing the birds, and getting fresh air and sunshine does a body good. I also refuse to eat fast food or junk food. Since my time is limited, I often prepare a big pot of soup that we can eat for several days. I do the same with spaghetti sauce and other meal staples. I always have fresh fruit in the fridge for healthy snacking. Also, don't forget to hydrate; our bodies require a lot of water.

Fourth, we flourish by trusting in God's faithful love, which endures forever and ever. That means we don't stop. It means we remember His faithful love and remember that He is faithfully with us and for us. It means that on hard days, we trust His love will support us. On long days, we trust His faithful love will sustain us.

My fervent hope is that these disciplines will help you to flourish emotionally, spiritually, and physically.

A CAREGIVER PRAYER

Lord, I long to flourish emotionally, spiritually, and physically while I live the caregiver's life. Will You please help me to incorporate any necessary changes, by Your grace? Give me a willing heart and guide me by showing me which of the above I will benefit from the most. Help me start small without feeling overwhelmed, and help me avoid procrastination.

Please provide someone I can share my feelings with and pray with. Please help me make it to church and devote time to read Your Word daily. May it strengthen and support me. Help me to move my body and eat healthy, whole foods instead of junk. And help me never to stop trusting in Your faithful love. In Jesus's name, amen.

THOUGHTS FOR TODAY

+ It is possible to flourish emotionally, spiritually, and physically.
+ I will ask God to help me flourish and then do my part.
+ I will open my Bible and read it daily.

MY THOUGHTS AND PRAYERS

_____

_____

_____

_____

_____

_____

DAY SIX
A FRESH ATTITUDE

And be constantly renewed in the spirit of your mind [having a
fresh mental and spiritual attitude].
—Ephesians 4:23 AMPC

Everything changes when we become caregivers. We wave goodbye to tidy, reasonable schedules, white hankies waving, as the ins and outs of our mere lives are radically altered. Sometimes, this might involve bedrooms becoming playrooms or living rooms becoming life care centers. This may mean counters filled with medicine bottles or fridges filled with baby bottles. Sometimes, it may mean accompanying loved ones on frequent trips to and from the hospital.

Bumpy weeks become the norm as, by necessity, our outside activities are curtailed. Life shrinks. For me, one of the most difficult aspects of caregiving has been the shrinking of my personal and mental space. Adjustments and flexibility are essential, and for those of us who crave order or even just miss our regular lives, this can be an emotionally tough time. It's challenging to embrace and adapt to a new normal. Finding our footing during this journey is a real struggle.

Constant change, constant flexibility, and constant interruptions require massive amounts of God's grace. The good news is that through His Spirit and His Word, we can experience the continuous renewal of our minds (as Ephesians 4:23 says above), which makes all the difference. As we purpose in our hearts to accept and surrender to the caregiving period that God has brought into our lives, we must deeply breathe in His Word, which is living and active (see Hebrews 4:12), allowing it to inform, strengthen, equip, and sustain us.

Today's key verse showcases the vital importance of our attitude. The continual change in our lives requires a constant renewal of our minds. It requires a fresh mental and spiritual attitude. One that reacts far differently, far more graciously. This only happens by God's grace as we cry out for what we desperately need. When my attitude stinks, my day spirals—fast. Those around me wilt, and God is not honored. But when I treasure His Word, humbly acknowledging the need for my mind to be constantly renewed and my dire need for a fresh mental and spiritual attitude, then the very thing I cannot do is what God's grace swoops in to accomplish.

A CAREGIVER PRAYER

Lord, since I have been caregiving, so much has changed in my life. As the weeks bump by, help me to be flexible, adjust my routines and my expectations, and embrace the new normal that You have orchestrated. I confess I have not always had a good attitude about it. Please forgive me and help me to navigate the changes with a fresh mental and spiritual attitude, by Your grace. I humbly acknowledge my need for Your Word to transform my mind and my thinking. Help me to treasure Your Word and allow it entrance into my heart. May it bear much fruit in my life as through it I am strengthened, equipped, and sustained in this season of constant change.

As I care for my loved one, thank You for helping me to be regularly renewed in the spirit of my mind. In Jesus's name, amen.

THOUGHTS FOR TODAY

- ✦ I don't have to navigate jarring changes on my own.
- ✦ I can possess a fresh mental and spiritual attitude.
- ✦ God's Word strengthens, equips, and sustains me.

MY THOUGHTS AND PRAYERS

_____

_____

_____

_____

_____

_____

DAY SEVEN
SOUL PROCESSING WITH GOD

To you, O Lord, I lift up my soul. O my God, in you I trust.
—Psalm 25:1–2 esv

One thing I quickly learned to do while caregiving (not because I'm brilliant, but more out of desperation) was to acknowledge to myself, and especially to the Lord, all that I was experiencing inwardly. I discovered that instead of bearing alone avalanches of sorrow that made my heart shiver, I could instead cry out in my anguish and be heard and comforted by my safe, loving, good heavenly Father. And this has made all the difference.

Had I not practiced this essential, encouraging stance/prayer, all the knots in my heart and all the dark spaces in my soul might have suffocated me. They certainly would have hindered me on days when I cared for a whimpering, feverish baby. On days when my sixty-year-old body fought illness without opportunity for rest. On seemingly endless, exhausting days.

King David, in Psalm 25 (and many other psalms), models the beauty of honesty before the Lord. Verses one and two, in particular, have enabled me to release whatever is most pressing on my heart and mind, acknowledging and releasing it to the Lord. When I say aloud (yes, I really do), *"To you, O Lord, I lift up my soul,"* I am revealing to almighty God what's inside me: the good, the bad, and the ugly. I am opening myself up to Him, lifting my inner self to Him, in a plea for help. I am saying, "God, You see the battered, hurting parts. You see the exhaustion. You see the fear and the uncertainty."

But this section of Scripture doesn't end there, and neither do I. I then go on to say aloud, *"O my God, in you I trust."* This portion of the verse-turned-prayer is essential because it pivots my heart away from all that entangles it and positions it toward the One who is faithful and trustworthy. When we declare with our mouth that we trust our heavenly Father, we are reminding ourselves that we can, should, and must trust Him in this caregiving journey. Sometimes, that is a daily choice. Sometimes, it's a minute-by-minute choice.

This beautiful passage, when used by us as a prayer, facilitates openness and transparency before the Lord, enables us to relinquish our heavy caregiving loads to our faithful God, and reminds our tender souls that, ultimately, we can and do trust in Him.

A CAREGIVER PRAYER

Lord, please help me to learn to be open, honest, and transparent with You by lifting up my soul whenever I feel stressed or overwhelmed by caregiving duties. Help me not to carry the heavy burden that You never intended for me to deal with alone. I'm grateful that You are safe, kind, good, and loving, and I can safely bare my soul to You every time I feel the need.

Help me to remember that You are faithful and utterly trustworthy, and I can relinquish and entrust every single concern to You. I can and do trust You, Lord, to hear me, strengthen me, encourage me, and help me. "To you, O LORD, I lift up my soul. O my God, in you I trust." In Christ's name, amen.

THOUGHTS FOR TODAY

- I can acknowledge and release my most pressing concerns to the Lord.

- Being honest with the Lord helps me relinquish my heavy cares to Him.

- Ultimately, I can trust my heavenly Father, who listens to me and comforts me.

MY THOUGHTS AND PRAYERS

_____

_____

_____

_____

_____

_____

DAY EIGHT
YOU ARE KNOWN

If anyone loves God, he is known by him.
—1 Corinthians 8:3

Most of the caregiving we engage in is provided privately, without any raucous crowd or celebratory band or applause to cheer us on. In fact, because of all that is required of us, many of us often work by ourselves. It's easy to feel isolated and alone because, frequently, we are. That's why it's essential to schedule regular times of reprieve, if possible—to get out on occasion, to talk with a friend, to relax, to take walks and read books, as God provides help and as we are able.

However, it's also significant to understand the life-changing truth that when we love God, we are known by Him. We are known in a way that even a cherished friend or our beloved spouse can never truly understand. I think God arranged it that way so that our hopes and expectations would never be pinned on a specific person—however loving and kind—but on the One who alone knows us on a level not humanly possible.

Today's verse declares that when we love God, we are known by Him—truly known. That means He knows the number of hairs on our heads (see Luke 12:7), and He knows our hearts, knows all that ricochets through our taxed minds, and knows our inner struggles. God Himself witnesses all our efforts. He is not oblivious to our current, sometimes-chaotic, caregiving schedule. He knows how hard we're trying, and He knows our sacrifices. He also knows the turmoil and grief that sometimes rise up in our hearts.

How wonderful and encouraging to be so intimately known by our good, loving, and kind heavenly Father. What a relief to realize that we aren't alone, after all. Because being known by God implies that He is with us. In fact, God reassures us that He is *always* with us. He has said, *"I will never leave you or abandon you"* (Hebrews 13:5).

How awesome that, as we work and whisper our fervent requests to the One we love, He stands near and hears us. The One who knows us so well envelops us with His presence and equips us with His grace. And I wholeheartedly believe He is cheering us on.

A CAREGIVER PRAYER

Thank You, Father, that you know those who love You. Lord, I do love You, and my heart swells with gratitude that You intimately know me inside and out. You know the number of hairs on my head, and You know my heart. You know my struggles, You know how hard I am working, and You know my sometimes-chaotic thoughts and schedule. Lord, will You please provide a way for me to have occasional reprieve?

As I work in private and days of isolation stretch on, I'm so grateful that, even then, I am not truly alone because You never leave me. You are near, You hear every whispered prayer, and You cover me with Your presence. Thank You for Your amazing grace as I help my loved one. Help me to remember that You are cheering me on. In Jesus's name, amen.

THOUGHTS FOR TODAY

+ I love God, and I am truly and intimately known by Him.

+ God is not oblivious to my schedule but knows my efforts and struggles.

+ I am not alone; God envelops me with His presence.

MY THOUGHTS AND PRAYERS

_____

_____

_____

_____

_____

_____

DAY NINE
OVERFLOWING WITH HOPE

*Now may the God of hope fill you with all joy and peace
as you believe so that you may overflow with hope by the power
of the Holy Spirit.*
—Romans 15:13

Several years ago, I hosted a morning Bible study for the women of our church. Many wonderful women showed up at my home week after week, and as we talked and laughed, munching on donut holes and fresh strawberries, one woman in particular stood out to me. Maggie, as I'll refer to her, didn't always show up. However, I was continuously impressed with her hope-filled attitude on the weeks she walked through my front door. This astonished me because Maggie's daughter was, much to her deep grief, a drug addict. As a result, Maggie, in her mid-to-late sixties, had full custody of her grandchildren—all five of them, including a newborn.

Maggie's situation astonishes me even more now that I have spent the last four years caring for our granddaughter while our single daughter works full-time. Maggie's load was heavy. It was certainly not her plan, nor was it something she would have preferred. Despite the circumstances, Maggie's hope was built on her prayers and on her deep love for the Lord.

Years later, when it became apparent that I would soon be called into a similar role (we are not raising our granddaughter but caring for her during her mother's full-time work hours), I remembered Maggie's can-do attitude. By God's grace, I, too, have managed to hold on to hope. Hope that I will make it through. Hope that God will give me continued strength and grace. Hope that, ultimately, God's plan and purpose will unfold, and that I can trust Him in the process, even though it is vastly different from my plans.

How encouraging to know that our heavenly Father is not the God of despair but the God of hope. We serve the God of hope— who also wants us and our loved ones to walk in hope! As we believe Him, with eyes and hearts focused on Him rather than on all we're enduring in this caregiving journey, He fills us with all joy and peace. *All* joy. *All* peace. *All* ours. Why? So that through the power of His Holy Spirit, we may overflow with hope.

A CAREGIVER PRAYER

Lord, You are the God of hope, and I am grateful. I am grateful that I can trust You amid sometimes-baffling situations, knowing that, ultimately, Your plans and purposes will prevail in my life and in the life of my loved one. Help me, by Your grace, to keep my eyes and heart focused on You and not on all the difficulties that often surround me.

Help me to maintain my hope by trusting You more. Thank You for filling me with all joy and all peace, as I believe that You are sovereign, good, and kind. May my heart daily overflow with hope by the power of Your Holy Spirit, and may I daily walk in the strength and reassurance Your hope gives me. In Jesus's name, amen.

THOUGHTS FOR TODAY

- I serve the God of hope.

- God gives me all joy and all peace as I believe Him.

- I have hope because I trust that God's purpose and plan always prevail.

MY THOUGHTS AND PRAYERS

_____

_____

_____

_____

_____

_____

DAY TEN
NO COMPARISON

For I consider that the sufferings of this present
time are not worth comparing with the glory that is
going to be revealed to us.
—Romans 8:18

When my beloved Gram's time on earth drew close to its end, I sat next to her in her hospital room on a plastic chair, scooted close to her bed, and bent forward so I could rest my hand atop hers. Oh, how I longed for another conversation, for more laughs, for more time together. More like a mother than a grandmother to me, she and my grandfather had hosted me for countless happy, safe summer weeks while I was growing up. Watching her suffer made my heart constrict, and I gulped deep, calming breaths as I prayed for her.

When those we love suffer, our hearts ache on their behalf. That's part of what makes caregiving so difficult. Of course, we do the best we can; we focus on the next thing that needs to be accomplished, and we offer measures of comfort, like pillows, smiles, and quiet words of encouragement. But whether we are helping in a hospice situation, with long-term physical needs, or with caring for little ones, the pain in our hearts over the situation (and our lack of control over it) can be intensely agonizing.

Yet pain serves a purpose in God's economy, and one of the things it does is help us, as believers, to look forward to the time hinted at in Romans 8:18. What I love about this verse is that the apostle Paul does not sugarcoat or ignore the reality that suffering happens. No one is immune to pain. This is a priceless, divine perspective and is itself a gift. But, of course, the primary message of this verse is that, in comparison, all our earthly suffering will never hold a candle to the magnificence of an eternity with Jesus and all that awaits us in heaven.

As we watch our loved one suffer and it takes its toll on us, we can remember that, for those who know Jesus, pain is not indefinite, and all suffering is temporary. Revelation 21:4 beautifully assures us, *"He will wipe away every tear from their eyes. Death will be no more; grief, crying, and pain will be no more, because the previous things have passed away."*

There is waiting for us an unimaginable glory, wrapped in Christ's triumph, that is beyond our ability to comprehend. But it exists. I can scarcely fathom experiencing life without sorrow, tears, or pain. However, the truth is that one day, I will. So will you. And there will be no comparison.

A CAREGIVER PRAYER

Lord, You see how my heart aches as I walk this caregiving journey. Some days, the pain feels almost unbearable. Will You please encourage and comfort me? Remind me to hold fast to the divine perspective that suffering happens on this earth, that no one is immune, and that there is coming a glory that will make all I'm enduring pale in comparison.

Help me to focus on the truth that, because of the finished work of the cross, one day, there will be no more tears, grief, crying, pain, or death. Remind me by Your Spirit that all suffering is temporary and that, one day, I will experience unimaginable glory. In Jesus's name, amen.

THOUGHTS FOR TODAY

+ Suffering happens on earth; no one is immune.

+ My current pain is providing me with a priceless perspective.

+ One day, I will experience the glory of new life, without pain, sorrow, grief, or tears.

MY THOUGHTS AND PRAYERS

_____

_____

_____

_____

_____

_____

DAY ELEVEN
DON'T BE AFRAID OR DISCOURAGED

Haven't I commanded you: be strong and courageous?
Do not be afraid or discouraged, for the Lord your God is with
you wherever you go.
—Joshua 1:9

For many of us, caregiving is the mountain we didn't realize we'd be climbing, the adventure we never anticipated experiencing, with demands we never imagined fulfilling. It can be a scary position, fraught with uncertainties about how life works now, along with legitimate concerns about our ability to meet so many (often new) challenges.

I wonder if Joshua felt similarly when, after Moses's death, he transitioned from assisting Moses to leading the Israelites. If God's words to Joshua in today's key verse are any indication, then, clearly, Joshua struggled with both fear and discouragement. Maybe he wondered if the Israelites would honor him as they did Moses. Or perhaps he wrestled with whether he was up to the task. Either way, the Lord saw Joshua's heart and spoke many words of encouragement to his soul.

So, lead he did. Joshua led his countrymen in treading new ground across the Jordan River. Like many of us on our caregiving journey, he was in unfamiliar territory. Joshua recognized this fact and explained to his countrymen, *"For you haven't traveled this way before"* (Joshua 3:4).

Many of us are, likewise, on new ground, in uncharted territory. The only way we can navigate it successfully is through God's grace. The beauty of Joshua 1:9 isn't that God commands Joshua to *"be strong and courageous."* It's not that God says, *"Don't be afraid or discouraged."* I'm sure Joshua knew what he should and shouldn't do (same for us!). Instead, the beauty of this verse is that God provides the answer to "How?"

How, exactly, can we be strong and courageous? How can we stop ourselves from being afraid or discouraged? By resting in the absolute fact that the Lord our God is with us wherever we go. Knowing God Himself is with us changes everything. We don't have to manufacture courage. As we walk in places we've never been before, almighty God, Maker of heaven and earth, equips us with grace and gives us strong, bold, very courageous hearts.

A CAREGIVER PRAYER

Lord, as I face the caregiving days ahead, help me not to be afraid or discouraged. Though I may not have foreseen this path, Your grace is truly sufficient and enables me to serve in this manner and to continue serving. I lift all my concerns to You and trust You to give me the energy, strength, and stamina I need daily.

Thank You, Lord, that You are with me on every step of this caregiving path. Thank You that I am not alone and that You equip me with Your great grace and Your reassuring, strengthening presence. I rejoice that I don't have to manufacture courage, but I can take courage because You are with me. Thank You for equipping me with a strong, bold, very courageous heart. In Jesus's name, amen.

THOUGHTS FOR TODAY

+ As I walk this new path, God gives me great grace.

+ Almighty God is with me wherever I go.

+ God equips me and makes me strong, bold, and very courageous.

MY THOUGHTS AND PRAYERS

_____

_____

_____

_____

_____

DAY TWELVE
BREAK UP WITH WORRY

Therefore don't worry about tomorrow, because tomorrow will worry about itself. Each day has enough trouble of its own.
—Matthew 6:34

Confession: I have lain awake at night, my mind sprinting, my body tense, my heart overwhelmed, sleeping little and picturing every worst-case scenario imaginable, all thanks to my not-so-good friend, worry. This rude acquaintance loves to whisper all the bad things that could occur. It reminds me of all the negative what-ifs. It taunts me from restful sleep to full-blown, uneasy insomnia.

Obviously, I don't have a friend (more like foe) called Worry, but it has certainly felt that way at times. I have discovered that the key to dodging this foe is twofold: prayer and trust. I have learned to humbly kneel next to my bed each night, lifting up every concern—legitimate or trivial. I have learned to relinquish every iota of worry and every catastrophic scenario lurking deep in the back of my mind to the One who listens and lifts it away. I have learned to cry out to my good heavenly Father, who always hears, and to fully vent every heavy worry in my heart and mind. And you can do the same—in fact, you must. The only way to avoid being overwhelmed by our burdens in this caregiving season is to ask the Lord to take them. He will.

After we have relinquished every last worry and thought, our next step is to trust the One who is faithful and utterly trustworthy. We must choose to believe that He is with us and that He will help us. We must choose to trust that He is faithful and that He will do what we cannot. *"He who calls you is faithful; he will do it"* (1 Thessalonians 5:24).

Leaving our worries in God's hands and trusting Him to help us sounds so inviting. However, the reality of walking it out can be challenging. This is where we engage our faith. This is where we choose to not only hear Jesus's words in today's key verse but to actually believe and do them. It's then that we'll truly, once and for all, finally end our friendship with worry.

A CAREGIVER PRAYER

Lord, I confess all the times I have worried instead of praying and trusting You, and, oh, Lord, it has cost me peace. When worries bombard my mind and heart, please give me the grace to turn every concern, every worst-case scenario, every dread into a prayer of relinquishment. Help me to give every single apprehension fully to You.

And Lord, help me to trust You. As I care for my loved one, may faith arise in my heart as I read Your Word. May I choose not to worry but instead trust You fully. God, You are faithful. You are utterly trustworthy. I choose to believe that You are with me and that You will do what I cannot. In Jesus's name, amen.

THOUGHTS FOR TODAY

- When tempted to worry, I will instead pray and trust God.

- My prayers should include every worst-case scenario and every single concern.

- I will walk in faith, choose to trust God, and end my friendship with worry.

MY THOUGHTS AND PRAYERS

_____

_____

_____

_____

_____

_____

DAY THIRTEEN
INFUSED WITH STRENGTH

I can do everything through Christ, who gives me strength.
—Philippians 4:13 NLT

When my four-year-old granddaughter attempts to open our sturdily locked patio door, she can instantly melt into hot tears of frustration. She pushes, bangs, and twists the handle (and sometimes kicks the door), to no avail. Hearing her wails, I'll stoop down next to her and say, "Do you need help? You don't have to cry and bang. Just ask." Much to her relief, the door is unlocked, and she can once again play on the back porch.

Don't we sometimes act the same? Our best efforts frustrate us and those around us. We wear ourselves out when all we have to do is ask for help. Yet we leave the One for whom nothing is impossible right out of the equation. We struggle, push, bang, and make every effort imaginable, completely forgetting about asking Jesus for His help. If, apart from Him, we can do nothing (see John 15:5), then why do we attempt so much without His most needed assistance? Whether through forgetfulness, a lack of awareness of our need for His help, or even pride, the outcome is the same: a serious lack of results, exhaustion, and frustration.

When we stop, humble ourselves, and choose to pray and ask for His help, Christ unlocks the most sturdily locked door, easing the way for us and enabling us to succeed in our tasks. I love the *Amplified Bible, Classic Version* of Philippians 4:13: "*I have strength for all things in Christ Who empowers me [I am ready for anything and equal to anything through Him Who infuses inner strength into me; I am self-sufficient in Christ's sufficiency].*"

We truly have the capacity to be good caregivers, regardless of our situation, when Christ empowers us. Long-term or short-term, whether ushering a loved one to heaven or ushering a brand-new life into the world, wherever our help is needed, through Christ, we can meet every challenge. We are ready for anything. Equal to anything. Not because we're able but because He empowers us. God designed it this way so that our hearts would never fully depend on ourselves but would firmly rely on Him who infuses us with inner strength.

A CAREGIVER PRAYER

Lord, forgive me for neglecting to ask for Your help as I care for my loved one. Give me a humble heart that recognizes my deep need for Your strength in all I attempt. Help me to meet every challenge by Your grace and in Your strength, not by my own.

Help me to start the holy habit of asking for Your help as soon as I awaken, for truly, Lord, apart from You, I can do nothing. Thank You, Lord, that when You equip me with strength, I am ready for anything and equal to everything. May I remember this daily and depend on You. In Jesus's name, amen.

THOUGHTS FOR TODAY

+ When I'm frustrated, all I have to do is ask Jesus for His help.

+ I really do have the capacity to be a good caregiver when Christ empowers me.

+ Through Christ, I am ready for anything and equal to anything.

MY THOUGHTS AND PRAYERS

_____

_____

_____

_____

_____

_____

DAY FOURTEEN
GOD HIMSELF HELPS YOU

*The Lord God will help me; therefore I have not been
humiliated; therefore I have set my face like flint,
and I know I will not be put to shame.*
—Isaiah 50:7

If you've asked yourself, "How on earth is this whole caregiving thing possibly going to work?" or wondered, "Do I even have the capacity to meet this current need?" I can relate. When our single daughter became pregnant and chose to keep her baby, initially, I had no clue how drastically it would affect our lives. We adore our granddaughter and praise God for her little life. But the adjustment to care for her so her mom could earn a living was a major life change, filled with stresses and adjustments on many levels.

Thankfully, the Lord God did indeed help me. He helped my husband, Keith, and me, giving us grace, strength, and wisdom to navigate the changes and help our daughter and granddaughter in myriad ways. He reassured our often anxious, often weary hearts and strengthened us to the degree that we knew—we absolutely knew—we were in this for the long haul.

When circumstances arise over which we have no control, it is such a relief to know that we don't manage the fallout on our own. Trusting that God Himself is aware of all we're facing and that in His great kindness and power, He helps us, is huge. God's help equips us with everything that each situation requires. His help enables us to stand, think clearly, make adjustments, and even enjoy our new, challenging place. (Yes, that can actually happen!)

As almighty God helps us, He also enables us to see this season with a fresh perspective. Yes, a caregiving season is a life-altering season. To be honest, it interrupts our daily lives, inconveniences us, and essentially transforms the way we live. And yet, it also brings us great joy and a huge blessing in the lives of our loved ones. Despite the difficulties, there are also frequent, beautiful moments of joy. Joy to meet a very real need. Joy to give of ourselves to a degree that we otherwise might never have managed. And joy to literally be Jesus's hands and feet.

A CAREGIVER PRAYER

Lord, when I am overwhelmed by the prospect of all that lies ahead of me, wondering if I even have the capacity to meet the many needs I see, I'm grateful that I don't have to manage everything on my own because You, my faithful God, help me. You help me to stand; You give me grace and wisdom to navigate every change and help me meet every need.

As I face the interruptions and inconveniences that this season has brought into my daily life, it gives me a fresh perspective. Thank You for making me a huge blessing in the life of my loved one. Bless me with moments of joy as I tend to every task, remembering that in this season, You are allowing me to be Jesus's hands and feet. In His name, amen.

THOUGHTS FOR TODAY

+ The Lord God will help me in every situation.

+ God gives me fresh perspective and makes me a blessing.

+ God gives me the joy of being Jesus's hands and feet.

MY THOUGHTS AND PRAYERS

_____

_____

_____

_____

_____

_____

HE SHIELDS US

*But you, LORD, are a shield around me, my glory, and the one
who lifts up my head.*
—Psalm 3:3

When we're in the trenches of caregiving, laying down our lives for a period of time to assist in whatever way is needed, battles of all sorts can play out in our minds. Here are a few of the mental and emotional skirmishes we might face.

The Battle of Resentment: This is the place where our mind dwells when we're not fully surrendered to God's current call on our lives. We dislike the arduous work involved, the changes we couldn't avoid, and the fact that our once comfortable, normal life has been disrupted. Maybe we're upset because no one else has stepped up.

The Battle of Self-Pity: This occurs when our perception becomes distorted, and we perceive ourselves as the victims in the entire scenario. We have our own issues, goals, and lives. This whole caregiving stint has interfered with them and caused untold stress, weariness, and aggravation. In the battle of self-pity, it's truly all about us.

The Battle of Discouragement: When life is intense, and we're exhausted, we sometimes neglect to resist the enemy until he encroaches into our minds and pulls us straight down. Our hearts sag, and we begin to lose hope. Soon, we're wallowing in utter discouragement, certain we're scarcely able to keep up with the demands.

But God lifts our heads! And the Lord is our shield, encircling our minds and hearts. He gives us grace to:

Resist resentment by surrendering afresh to our current season (daily, if necessary!), trusting that we are exactly where we're supposed to be—in the center of God's will. There's no better place!

Resist self-pity as we recognize that supporting our loved one is a temporal assignment and a huge blessing. When we generously refresh others, we, too, are refreshed. *"The generous will prosper; those who refresh others will themselves be refreshed"* (Proverbs 11:25 NLT).

Resist discouragement by giving us the wisdom to take care of ourselves so we're not as susceptible to the enemy's attacks. When we humble ourselves, accepting the position where God has currently placed us, and we then resist the devil, he must flee (see James 4:7), and our hearts are encouraged.

A CAREGIVER PRAYER

Thank You, Lord, that You are a shield around me. You are my glory, and You lift up my head. Give me the grace to recognize the battles and temptations into which the enemy is trying to draw me. Help me to realize that in my frail humanity, I seriously need to cry out to You, submit to You, and resist the enemy so that he flees from me.

Give me the grace to surrender daily to You so that I resist resentment. Give me the grace to see my current assignment as a blessing, and refresh me, so that I resist self-pity. Give me the wisdom to care for myself, especially now, so that I'm not too worn down mentally and physically to resist the enemy. In Jesus's name, amen.

THOUGHTS FOR TODAY

+ I resist resentment by surrendering afresh to God's plan.

+ I resist self-pity by seeing my assignment as a blessing.

+ I resist discouragement by taking care of myself, submitting to God, and resisting the devil.

MY THOUGHTS AND PRAYERS

_____

_____

_____

_____

_____

_____

DAY SIXTEEN
SIMPLE BUT MIGHTY HABITS

He restores my soul. He leads me in paths of righteousness for his name's sake.
—Psalm 23:3 ESV

While my husband recovered from his second hip replacement surgery, I was still caring for our then-two-year-old granddaughter, and I grew physically exhausted. Worse, I grew spiritually weary. As caregivers, we will walk through deep valleys unique to our situation. Hard days happen. Sometimes, difficult seasons last longer than we hoped. King David knew these valleys well, prompting him to pen these words: *"Even though I walk through the valley of the shadow of death, I will fear no evil, for you are with me"* (Psalm 23:4 ESV).

The time we spend caring for our loved one can sometimes feel excessively taxing and even bleak. Be aware that this can take a spiritual toll. It can lead us to spiritual lethargy or even spiritual exhaustion—where we simply don't have a prayer left in us. We're spiritually depleted.

We will do well to remember that taking care of others is demanding work. This path that He has led us on, for His name's sake, is a costly one. Just as a rancher or a construction worker requires regular, solid, and healthy meals to maintain their physical strength, we as caregivers need consistent, nourishing, and hearty spiritual sustenance.

There are simple but mighty habits that will sustain us on our worst days. One of these is to whisper regular prayers for help and strength. Another is to read our Bibles—daily. The book of Psalms, in particular, is a beautifully encouraging balm. Another simple but mighty habit is writing down a verse and committing it to memory so that we can draw on it when our hands are full and our days are demanding. If we don't give our weary souls the spiritual sustenance this current season demands, how can we expect to maintain our spiritual strength? How can we care for, lift, and encourage our loved one without first asking the Lord to care for, lift, and encourage us?

"He restores my soul." Let's remember that in all of this, Christ restores. *He* does this. We cannot do this. Our spouse cannot do this. Our best friend cannot. *He* restores our souls. While we are working on this holy assignment He has entrusted to us, we can do our part by praying and reading His Word. Then, we can rest in the fact that Jesus Himself will faithfully and continually restore our souls.

A CAREGIVER PRAYER

Lord, when days are especially demanding, make me alert and aware that this current, challenging assignment can take a spiritual toll, and this requires spiritual nourishment. Help me to do my part by praying throughout my day, asking for Your grace and strength, and encouraging my own heart and soul so I can do the same for my loved one.

Give me the grace to regularly engage in the simple but mighty habits of praying and reading Your Word. Give me the grace to memorize a passage that will lift my heart when my hands are occupied. Thank You, Lord, that You restore my soul as I do the work before me. In Jesus's name, amen.

THOUGHTS FOR TODAY

+ Be aware that caregiving is taxing and can take a spiritual toll.

+ This season requires regular, solid, spiritual sustenance.

+ Simple but mighty habits include praying and reading God's Word, which sustain me.

MY THOUGHTS AND PRAYERS

_____

_____

_____

_____

_____

_____

DAY SEVENTEEN
A PEACE-FILLED MIND

You will keep the mind that is dependent on you in perfect peace, for it is trusting in you.
—Isaiah 26:3

As I have spoken with other caregivers, several common threads have stood out to me. First, we've all faced the major life upheaval that came with taking on this task. Second, most of us are far more physically tired than normal (also, most of us no longer have a "normal"). However, there is a striking common denominator in a caregiver's life that resonates with many: a deep longing for peace. Part of this is because caregiving typically doesn't have a firm end date. It can feel like our lives are in limbo, and, to a degree, that's true. Plus, caregiving also has ripple effects, meaning it not only affects us but also impacts those closest to us. And, finally, it seems there are always multiple concerns (which can feel strangely like juggling) that threaten to steal our peace.

While all of these issues are true and legitimate, that doesn't mean peace must be an ever-elusive goal we can never quite attain. God shows us through His Word a solid way to hold on to peace in the most trying times: *"You will keep the mind that is dependent on you in perfect peace, for it is trusting in you."* Today's verse is like a peace promise. When we keep our minds dependent on almighty God—not on circumstances, not on results, not on how things are or are not progressing—He will keep our minds in perfect peace. The Lord does this because we're trusting Him. We're relying on Him to help us, to enable us, and to hold us in His perfect peace despite the uncertainty around us.

"You will keep…." This is the Lord's job, not ours. It's not up to us to hold ourselves in peace, and that's a good thing. *He* is the one who keeps our minds at peace as we depend on Him and trust Him amid

all our whirling concerns. He knows all the challenges we're facing and rewards our dependent trust with calm, clear, peaceful minds. What a beautiful gift!

A CAREGIVER PRAYER

Lord, You see all the legitimate concerns I consistently encounter as I care for my loved one. I lift each concern to You and ask for the grace to keep my mind dependent on You rather than fixated on my concerns. Help me to trust You as I do my best, by Your grace, to handle each task as it appears.

Thank You for Your promise of peace. Give me the grace to trust You and focus on You each day, committing my thoughts and mind more and more to Your Word. Teach me to keep my mind dependent on You, and as I do, thank You for the beautiful gift of Your peace filling my mind. In Jesus's name, amen.

THOUGHTS FOR TODAY

+ Peace is not an ever-elusive goal; peace is attainable for me.

+ I can trust God throughout my day and keep my mind dependent on Him.

+ As I trust God and focus on Him, He *will* give me a peaceful mind.

MY THOUGHTS AND PRAYERS

_____

_____

_____

_____

_____

_____

CALM IN OUR STORM

He got up, rebuked the wind, and said to the sea, "Silence! Be
still!" The wind ceased, and there was a great calm.
—Mark 4:39

Last night, our city was hit by 80 mph winds thanks to Hurricane Helene, a Category 4 storm that roared onto Florida's Big Bend coast. We don't live in Florida. But the massive storm's bands stretched out more than 350 miles, clobbering much of the southeastern US with high winds and sideways rain long after dark.

Tornado sirens sounded at least a half dozen times before we went to bed. I wondered how on earth I'd sleep. But my husband, Keith, and I stopped and prayed for all those in the storm's path, and we asked the Lord for mercy, that the strength and winds of the hurricane would diminish. We also prayed for peace and sound sleep.

Hours later, I awoke at four in the morning, astonished at the noise. The winds roared, our house vibrated, and the windows rattled. Surprisingly, I didn't feel fear. God allowed Hurricane Helene to continue its path of destruction, yet my heart remained calm. Though our Lord is certainly able to command the wind and the seas to be still, as He did for the disciples in the story from which today's verse is taken, He often allows the storms to rage and brings a great calm to our hearts instead.

Caregiving can feel like a storm over which we have no control. Whether or not we receive a warning, when the winds of change blow, our hearts often vibrate with alarm, and we can definitely feel rattled. Storm clouds of particularly taxing and challenging days rush in and rock the boat of our lives. Sometimes, it seems like we're about to go under!

When the storm is severe, and we're on the brink of sinking, we can cry out to Jesus, just like the disciples did: *"Teacher! Don't you care that we're going to die?"* (Mark 4:38).

Of course, Jesus cares. I am grateful that even though the Lord sometimes allows storms to burst into our lives, in His great kindness, He blesses us—His children—by either calming the storm or calming our hearts. Oh, Jesus, You are Lord of every storm!

A CAREGIVER PRAYER

Lord, I recognize that I don't really have control over the storms of this caregiving journey, but I choose to trust You when the wind and waves hit. Even on the hardest and most challenging days, when it feels like my boat is sinking, help me to cry out to You and sense that You are with me.

Thank You for either calming the storm that blows out of nowhere or calming me while it rages. May the most challenging winds and rains of change not overtake me because my trust is firmly in You. Thank You for consistently calming my heart in every storm. Jesus, You truly are Lord of every storm. In Your name, amen.

THOUGHTS FOR TODAY

+ When the winds roar, and my heart vibrates, Jesus cares.

+ Jesus will either calm the storm or calm my heart.

+ Jesus is Lord of every storm.

MY THOUGHTS AND PRAYERS

_____

_____

_____

_____

_____

_____

DAY NINETEEN
IT'S ALL FOR HIM

Whatever you do, do it from the heart,
as something done for the Lord and not for people, knowing
that you will receive the reward of an inheritance from the
Lord. You serve the Lord Christ.
—Colossians 3:23–24

My guess is that not a single one of us became a caretaker to be noticed or appreciated by others. We rose to the occasion, whether it was convenient or not, despite whatever misgivings and uncertainties we may have had. We most likely stepped up with the sincerest hope that we could meet a need, help ease suffering, or improve the quality of life for our loved one. By God's grace, we will do just that. Undoubtedly, as believers, we recognize that God has placed it in our hearts to make this commitment.

As I have cared for our little granddaughter over the past few years, I have strongly sensed that everything I have done—rocking her, potty training her, feeding her, taking her to the park, and reading books to her—has ultimately been for the Lord. Yes, we are a huge help to our daughter. Yes, our granddaughter needs us and reaps the benefits of our serving in this capacity (and truly, though sometimes trying, it is our joy). But in my heart, it has all been for Jesus. Many times, when completing a chore or task for the sake of my daughter or granddaughter, I have prayed, "Let her see Jesus in this."

There is immense value in knowing that when we serve others, if our hearts are in the right place, we ultimately serve the Lord. This honors and pleases Christ, whom we represent as we live the life of a caregiver. It's an amazing blessing to know that when we do all we do for Him, we will one day receive the reward of an inheritance from Him.

When doubts, fatigue, or struggles arise concerning our caregiving assignment, there is a deep sense of satisfaction and gratitude in knowing that the Lord sees our hearts and recognizes all our hard work. We aren't unnoticed by our Savior. He knows it's all for Him. Let's remind ourselves daily that it's not just our loved one we serve, but we serve the Lord Christ.

A CAREGIVER PRAYER

Lord, my heart's desire is that I will do all that I do in my current caregiving assignment from my heart to please and honor You, knowing that it's actually You I serve. Help me to represent You well. In the midst of my struggles and fatigue, may I have a deep sense of satisfaction in knowing You see all my hard work and are pleased.

Oh, Lord, thank You that as I do all things for Your sake, I can trust that I will receive the reward of an inheritance from You. May I have great joy in serving my loved one. Help me to remember, Jesus, that, ultimately, though I serve them, I really serve You. In Your name, amen.

THOUGHTS FOR TODAY

+ While I serve as a caregiver, I am ultimately serving the Lord.

+ The Lord sees and recognizes all of my hard work.

+ One day, I will receive the reward of an inheritance from the Lord.

MY THOUGHTS AND PRAYERS

_____

_____

_____

_____

_____

_____

DAY TWENTY
ON TRIALS AND ENDURANCE

Consider it a great joy, my brothers and sisters, whenever you experience various trials, because you know that the testing of your faith produces endurance.
—James 1:2–3

If we're honest, our caregiving journey—because it is indeed a journey—can be the source of much consternation. We don't understand (or like) why this situation (an illness, an accident, an unplanned birth) has happened. We don't know why healing hasn't occurred. We can't comprehend why the entire ordeal is taking so long. We don't grasp why our loved one is suffering to this degree (as we, by default, also suffer). And on and on.

Caring for our loved one is a trial, one of the various trials that James, the half-brother of Jesus, writes about in today's verse. Notice James doesn't say "if" you experience various trials, but "whenever." That's because trials are guaranteed to us on this earth. There's no avoiding them. No human on earth receives a "get out of trials *free*" card. Even Jesus endured trials!

James begins by urging us to consider the trials we experience as a great joy. For most of us, that's a tall order. I have never caught myself feeling especially joyful as a result of my caregiving journey. Should this be our goal? Is it possible? Can we truly gain a divine perspective on our trials that might lead to authentic joy?

James goes on to explain why we should consider our trials a great joy, and it is so interesting. He implies that trials are the testing of our faith. In other words, God allows suffering into our lives as an opportunity for us to grow in faith. Will we pass the test? Will we trust God through it? Do we see God's hand in it? Are we assured that He is with us and is helping us? Will we emerge on the other side, knowing and trusting Christ more, and reflecting His image more faithfully?

The end goal is for us to view the trials that test our faith as a joy. Not because they are joyful in themselves, but because they produce a most holy characteristic in those who are refined by them. Endurance. We're called to endure. As Jesus endured, as His disciples endured, so must we.

A CAREGIVER PRAYER

Lord, I want to see trials the way You do—as opportunities for great joy, chances to grow in faith, trust, and reliance on You, and tools for building endurance. I know that the testing of my faith produces endurance, and I know that I desperately need to endure through this caregiving journey and in my life. Please strengthen and help me. I cannot do this apart from You.

Will You please grant me a divine perspective and help me to embrace the very thing I naturally tend to shrink from? Help me to see trials as from You and to trust You in and through each one. As Jesus and His disciples endured, may I do the same, by Your great grace. In Jesus's name, amen.

THOUGHTS FOR TODAY

+ No human on earth gets a "get out of trials free" card.

+ I can learn to view my trials as opportunities for great joy.

+ As Jesus and His disciples endured, so must I.

MY THOUGHTS AND PRAYERS

_____

_____

_____

_____

_____

_____

DAY TWENTY-ONE
HIS HEART IS KIND

We give great honor to those who endure under suffering.
For instance, you know about Job, a man of great endurance.
You can see how the Lord was kind to him at the end, for the
Lord is full of tenderness and mercy.
—James 5:11 NLT

Because my earthly father struggled with rage and was emotionally unavailable during my life, my initial concept of a father was not necessarily a good or healthy one. After I became a Christian in my late twenties, I slowly began to understand the reality of our heavenly Father's kindness, goodness, and mercy. These truths have always surprised me, in a good way. It never occurred to me that God had so many good characteristics because I had no frame of reference, so I didn't expect it. As I continue to grow and mature in Christ, I continually uncover more of our heavenly Father's good characteristics, and I never cease to be amazed and delighted.

Several years ago, the lyrics of the song "10,000 Reasons (Bless the Lord)" by Matt Redman and Jonas Myrin, captured my heart. Over and over, I listened, astonished, as this song described the Lord's kind heart.

It particularly amazed and thrilled me to discover that God's heart is kind. What a priceless gift! What a loving heavenly Father! It amazes and thrills me that today's verse describes the Lord as "*full of tenderness and mercy.*" Oh, how deeply we need to know this—to drink it in like the parched gulping cool water.

Aren't these truths exactly what we need to live the life of a caregiver more effectively? Allowing these beautiful aspects of God's character to sink deep into our hearts is balm to our stressed, busy, often overwhelmed souls. There is healing and comfort that enables our inner selves to relax and be at ease, even while we care for our loved one. As the Lord's rich love, tenderness, and mercy wash over us, our hearts soften and are strengthened. With hearts made stronger and more compassionate, we're better equipped to love and serve well. Bless the Lord, O my soul!

A CAREGIVER PRAYER

Lord, will You please enable me to know You more accurately? To understand that as my heavenly Father, Your heart is kind and to know that You are full of tenderness and mercy? May Your rich love, tenderness, and mercy wash over me and change the way I see You and the way I engage as a caregiver.

May the truths about Your good character sink deep into my heart and heal, comfort, and transform me, even as I care for my loved one. And may this create ripple effects as I do my best to love and serve well in this season. In Jesus's name, amen.

THOUGHTS FOR TODAY

+ The Lord is full of tenderness and mercy.
+ My heavenly Father is slow to anger, and His heart is kind.
+ God's love, tenderness, and mercy wash over my heart, healing and equipping me.

MY THOUGHTS AND PRAYERS

_____

_____

_____

_____

_____

_____

DON'T STOP PRAYING

I love the Lord because he hears my voice
and my prayer for mercy. Because he bends down to listen,
I will pray as long as I have breath!
—Psalm 116:1–2 NLT

While visiting a new friend at her home, I noticed a small wooden plaque on the wall of her living room. It read: "Prayer changes things." It certainly does. Though God does not always answer in the manner or the timing we might prefer, He hears our prayers and responds.

Although God can and does do anything He desires and has no needs (see Acts 17:25), He has chosen to allow us, His dearly loved children, the right to petition Him, to cry out to Him, and to talk to Him through prayer whenever our hearts desire. Oh, that we would take advantage more often! Whether we're driving, preparing a meal, changing the bedsheets, or literally on our knees, this incredible, holy privilege must not be neglected. Through prayer, we are strengthened and encouraged, we gain wisdom, and we discern the next step. Through prayer, we are reassured and comforted, and can vent all our emotions (King David did this; just read the Psalms!).

If "*the prayer of a righteous person is very powerful in its effect*" (James 5:16), we must take advantage, especially as we help and serve our loved one in the caregiving role. How can we possibly hope to refrain from losing our temper, retain our joy, and maintain our stamina apart from God's help? And how will God help us if we don't ask Him in prayer?

In today's verse, God's incredible posture toward us is revealed; He is leaning in to hear the whispers of our hearts. Isn't that amazing? God *wants* to hear our words. Our heavenly Father longs to hear from us in the same way that we, as parents, long to hear about our children's day when they arrive home from school. Did you know that God delights in your prayers? He does. Proverbs 15:8 says, *"The prayer of the upright is his delight."*

In our verse for today, the psalmist goes on to declare that he will pray as long as he has breath. So should we! We can't afford to neglect this vital, holy habit. Feeling frustrated? Weary? Hopeless? Turn every one of those emotions into a prayer. God is bending toward you, waiting to hear every word.

A CAREGIVER PRAYER

Lord, I'm thankful that my prayers change things and that You bend toward me, waiting to hear every word I pray. I'm thankful that my prayers don't have to be eloquent or even make perfect sense, since You know and understand my heart.

Will You please give me the grace to turn every frustration, concern, grief, and emotion into prayer? Thank You for hearing my every whisper and for wanting to listen to me. Help me not to neglect the vital, holy habit of praying to You about everything. As long as I have breath, may I continue to cry out to You in prayer. In Jesus's name, amen.

THOUGHTS FOR TODAY

+ Prayer changes things.
+ Every emotion and situation can be turned into a prayer.
+ God is bending toward me, waiting to hear my prayers.

MY THOUGHTS AND PRAYERS

_____

_____

_____

_____

_____

DAY TWENTY-THREE
A HOPE-BASED REST

Rest in God alone, my soul, for my hope comes from him.
—Psalm 62:5

If there's one thing we caregivers need, it's rest. Although our assignments differ and some will last longer than others, I suspect that every one of us would raise our hands in the affirmative when asked if we need rest. Caregiving, by its nature, can be depleting. Draining. Especially if our situation appears hopeless.

God knew in advance the season we are now in. He isn't surprised by it and has prepared the way for us, even if it doesn't quite seem that way. Fortunately, there exists in God a hope-based rest for the weary soul.

Today's beautiful verse is a personal favorite. It reminds me that no matter what situation I face, how dire things seem, or how difficult the present moment is, my hope remains unshaken because it is not rooted in any of these temporal things. My hope is in God alone—the One who made the heavens and the earth, the One who created the glittering Milky Way galaxy, who flawlessly controls the seasons, and who formed each of us in our mother's womb.

Hope that is based on anything other than the almighty God is hope that cannot be sustained. But when our hope comes from Him and is in Him, our souls have true rest. This deep soul rest distinguishes itself from a mere nap, which, while nice, is not a long-term solution for a caregiver's weary heart. It distinguishes itself from the lack of pressures or problems (which, by the way, is impossible while we're on this spinning globe) and is, at best, temporary. This confident hope is based on faith and trust in God's faithfulness, trusting that He will see us through. Trusting in His goodness and His perfect character.

I have tucked this reassuring verse into my heart as a sweet reminder of what is true in those times when I sense a soul weariness sneaking up on me. Sometimes our souls need a good talking-to. When they do, we can tell them: Rest in God alone, my soul, for my hope comes from Him.

A CAREGIVER PRAYER

Lord, when I am involved in either ongoing or temporary circumstances that are unpleasant, hard, or frustrating, help me not to grow hopeless. May my hope not rest in any situation but, instead, may I place all of my hope in You. You are faithful and trustworthy. Enable me by Your great grace to keep my hope firmly fixed on You, so that I may experience genuine soul rest. Daily.

When necessary, help me to recognize when my soul needs a good talking-to. Please help me to tuck today's verse into my heart so that I can remind myself that my hope is not in the situation I'm facing but in You alone. In Jesus's name, amen.

THOUGHTS FOR TODAY

+ My hope is not in the temporal but in God alone.

+ Sometimes my soul needs a good talking-to.

+ When hope comes from God and is in God, I have true soul rest.

MY THOUGHTS AND PRAYERS

_____

_____

_____

_____

_____

TAKE A MOMENT

Let us not get tired of doing good, for we will reap at the proper
time if we don't give up.
—Galatians 6:9

After Hurricane Helene devastated our area, many trees fell onto power lines, leaving numerous people without power. By God's great mercy, my husband and I were not among them. Our son and his wife, who live twenty-five minutes away, did lose power and came to stay at our house until their power was eventually restored, five days later. Despite the stress such predicaments induce, our time together was enjoyable.

But the reality is that everyone's routine changed. We all had to make adjustments and allowances. Everyone did their best to accommodate one another. Yet. four days in, I felt overwhelmed. I can sometimes teeter emotionally when managing multiple issues, and as I continued to care for our granddaughter, planned a daily menu, and worked on this book, it all felt like too much.

Our caregiving journey can feel much the same way. As the comfort of our familiar routines evaporates and we juggle multiple issues—dealing with our own lives and commitments, as well as the logistics of helping our loved one—it can sometimes feel like too much.

The reality and responsibility of caring for an elderly loved one, an infirm family member, or a grandchild is daunting. The temptation to give up will always seem to arrive at our worst moments. (Of course!)

But we can't throw in the towel. We have to continue doing the good work that the Lord has assigned us. That day that I teetered emotionally? I took a moment, closed my bedroom door, took some deep breaths, and prayed. Specifically, I asked God for great grace to meet all the demands. I asked Him to refresh me and help me. And He did.

Sometimes we need to take a moment. Do some deep breathing. Pray—again—for grace and strength and for whatever else we need at that moment. This is how we persevere: not through human willpower, but through God's effusive grace and by His Spirit working in and through us, strengthening us, and helping us not to grow weary in doing good.

A CAREGIVER PRAYER

Lord, when my caregiving journey is plain hard, when the reality of all I am facing feels like too much, help me to remember to take a moment, breathe deeply, and pray for what I need right then. Please strengthen me in these moments. Encourage my heart. Help me to trust You for all I need so I won't grow weary and become tired of doing good.

Thank You for strengthening me, calming me, and helping me. Thank You that if I don't give up—and by Your grace I won't—I will reap. You see all I'm doing, and in the end, there is a reward. May I be a blessing to my loved one as I trust You to meet all of my own needs. In Jesus's name, amen.

THOUGHTS FOR TODAY

- The temptation to quit may come, but, by God's grace, I will keep going.
- I can take a moment, take a deep breath, and pray.
- Human willpower won't help me, but God's grace absolutely will.

MY THOUGHTS AND PRAYERS

_____

_____

_____

_____

_____

DAY TWENTY-FIVE
YOU ARE WELL-KNOWN BY GOD

Indeed, the hairs of your head are all counted. Don't be afraid;
you are worth more than many sparrows.
—Luke 12:7

Those of us who are mothers understand the wonder of holding our newborns, drinking in their sweet little faces, gazing at their precious little fingers and toes. Over the first few weeks of their lives, we scrutinize every fold of skin and either the peach fuzz on their little heads or, in my babies' case, all that dark hair standing straight up. We memorize every exquisite, soft, squirmy detail.

How incredible that God knows each of us to that same degree, and then some. He knows our hearts (see Luke 16:15 and Psalm 19:14, for starters), He understands our thoughts (see Psalm 139:2), and He is aware of all that we walk through (see Hebrews 4:13; Psalm 37:23).

More than two thousand years ago, Jesus spoke to a huge crowd, no doubt shocking them with a surprising and probably foreign thought: *"The hairs of your head are all counted."* Jesus shared that our heavenly Father knows us so intimately that He sees even this inconceivable detail. The idea of almighty God knowing us so well is a remarkable comfort. It means we're not at risk of being lost through the many cracks in this big, wide world. It means He knows our sometimes-complicated inner lives—our hearts, our emotions, and our struggles—far better than we do. And it means He understands us to a degree not humanly possible.

After Jesus spoke the above words, He told His followers not to be afraid and pointed out their great value. Our heavenly Father deeply loves and values us far more than any other part of His creation. This amazing fact produces courage in our hearts! We don't have to fear sharing anything with Him because He already knows it all!

As we care for our loved one today (and every day), let's drink in the amazing truth that God Himself knows the very number of hairs on our head. He knows all that troubles our hearts and the toll we sometimes bear emotionally. We aren't in this alone. He sees, He knows, and, when with great courage we pour out our hearts and requests to Him, He strengthens and equips us—His very well-known, well-loved children.

A CAREGIVER PRAYER

Lord, how remarkable that You know me to such a specific degree that You count the very number of hairs on my head! Thank You for deeply valuing and loving me and for seeing me as Your precious child. May these truths inspire great courage in my heart and enable me to pray with far greater transparency, because the truth is, You already know everything anyway.

I'm grateful that I will never fall through the cracks while I'm on this earth. As I walk through this caregiving journey, may these truths be a very real and solid comfort to my heart. Please help me think on these things and drink in Your love, today and always. In Jesus's name, amen.

THOUGHTS FOR TODAY

+ God knows my struggles, my heart, and the number of hairs on my head.

+ God understands my inner workings to a degree not humanly possible.

+ God deeply values and loves me.

MY THOUGHTS AND PRAYERS

_____

_____

_____

_____

_____

_____

DAY TWENTY-SIX
HIS MIGHTY ARMS NEVER FAIL

The eternal God is your dwelling place,
and underneath are the everlasting arms.
—Deuteronomy 33:27 ESV

Some hard days seem to last forever. Hard seasons can feel that way, too.

When Moses led the Israelites across the desert, he had no idea that what logistically should have been about an eleven-day trip would take four decades. However, during those decades, God guided His people and provided for their needs, including their hunger and thirst. In fact, despite the intense desert weather and their never-ending journey, the Israelites experienced two practical miracles, among many others, as indicated by Deuteronomy 29:5: *"I led you forty years in the wilderness; your clothes and the sandals on your feet did not wear out."*

Though they journeyed through scorching heat for years, their shoes didn't break. Thank God! Imagine, walking miles every day on burning desert sand. In addition, their clothes didn't fall apart. What a practical, loving example of God's faithful kindness to the Israelites, meeting their personal needs in a place without Walmart or Amazon delivery services. Similarly, God faithfully provides for our personal needs. He amply supplies energy and stamina for us as we (often wearily) hike through our caregiving journey.

As the years passed, Moses reminded the nomads he was leading that God Himself was their true dwelling place, their place of refuge and comfort. The same is true for us. Whether we've been caregiving for a brief stint or we're entering our fifth or our fifteenth year, wherever we currently find ourselves on our caregiver journey, it's tempting to believe that the demanding task in front of us will never end. Thank God that's not true. Thankfully, the day is coming when we will step into eternity and reside there, in our true home, forever with the eternal God.

We won't always struggle under extraordinarily heavy loads. Here on earth, we may struggle with long days, and sometimes with longer seasons than we would wish for, but eventually our part *will* be finished. In the meantime, the arms of almighty God are holding us up, and they will never fail us.

A CAREGIVER PRAYER

Lord, please grant me a humble heart and give me the grace to accept and surrender to my current caregiving reality. Help me to trust You, my sovereign Lord, in this season You have allowed in my life.

When the days are hard and I am physically weary, help me not to attempt to work in my feeble strength. Oh, Lord, will You please provide me with the energy and stamina I desperately need to match today's tasks? Thank You for meeting all my needs today and throughout this season.

When my days are long and the season I'm in feels like it will never end, help me to remember that's not true. You are my eternal God— please give me eternal perspective. Thank You that I can look forward to an eternal dwelling place with You. And thank You, Lord, for Your faithful, strong, everlasting arms, which always support me. In Jesus's name, amen.

THOUGHTS FOR TODAY

+ This season is not forever.

+ God can give me joy and satisfaction in this season.

+ God's mighty arms always support me.

MY THOUGHTS AND PRAYERS

DAY TWENTY-SEVEN
HOLD ON AND STOP IT

Peace I leave with you. My peace I give to you.
I do not give to you as the world gives.
Don't let your heart be troubled or fearful.
—John 14:27

Sometimes, on particularly demanding or unsettling days of caregiving, my soul likes to run off to the wild blue yonder, hooting and hollering like a crazy loon. It then frightens me with thoughts of worst-case scenarios, convinces me that all will soon be lost, and causes my heart to tremble.

When fear grips hard and won't let go, we do well to heed Jesus's words. Two parts of this section of Scripture stand out. The first one is instructional, warning us what not to do. I think Jesus says this to us because He knows how our souls are inclined: *"Don't let your heart be troubled or fearful."* The *Amplified Bible, Classic Edition* states it in much clearer terms: *"Stop allowing yourselves to be agitated and disturbed; and do not permit yourselves to be fearful and intimidated and cowardly and unsettled"* (John 14:27 AMPC).

This indicates that we have a choice. On our most overwhelming days, when our souls are taxed and we're inching closer to the ledge, Jesus basically says, "Stop it." The first time I read this verse, it was a true "lightbulb moment" for me. It seemed the Lord was coaching me, making me aware that I did not have to allow my soul to rev up or overreact. I could restrain it. I could walk in the fruit of the Spirit of self-control. (See Galatians 5:23.) I didn't have to allow myself to get all wound up. I didn't have to permit myself to be fearful and unsettled. What an empowering verse!

The second portion of today's verse that most stands out is Jesus offering us a priceless gift: *"Peace I leave with you. My peace I give to you."* The reason we can restrain our souls, stopping ourselves from freakouts and meltdowns, is because of His peace. He offers His unmatchable, priceless peace. All we need to do is accept it. Breathe it in. Hold on to it.

The next time your caregiving soul is tempted to fly off to the wild blue yonder and raise a ruckus, remember: hold on to Christ's peace. And stop it.

A CAREGIVER PRAYER

Lord, when demanding and unsettling days of caregiving hit hard, help me not to freak out, panic, melt down, or lose control. Help me not to let myself become agitated and unsettled. Help me not to borrow trouble and entertain worst-case scenarios. When upsets occur, may I consistently counsel my own heart with Your truth and choose to walk in the fruit of the Spirit, specifically self-control, instead of having freakouts and meltdowns.

Thank You for the priceless gift of Your peace, which holds me firm and secure in the most troubling moments. May I continually accept Your peace, breathe it in, and cling tightly to it. In Jesus's name, amen.

THOUGHTS FOR TODAY

+ I don't have to allow my heart to be troubled or fearful.

+ I can walk in the fruit of the Spirit of self-control.

+ I can restrain my soul and hold on to Christ's peace.

MY THOUGHTS AND PRAYERS

_____

_____

_____

_____

_____

_____

DAY TWENTY-EIGHT
BUSY HANDS, STILL HEARTS

Be still, and know that I am God.
—Psalm 46:10 ESV

There are many things we experience as caregivers. Stillness isn't typically one of them. With so many needs waiting to be met, most days we juggle multiple tasks, attend to urgent and immediate needs, and struggle to fit everything else in, such as prescriptions, appointments, and laundry, as time allows. Sometimes nonstop.

Case in point: As I've helped care for our precious granddaughter, I've rarely experienced an uninterrupted mealtime. Her requests certainly don't cease just because we're seated at the dinner table. (Especially during the potty-training phase.) Even now, with that process behind us, I juggle special requests ("I wanted the bunny plate!"), tears when a new food is viewed suspiciously, and occasional tantrums. Or I forgot the ranch dressing (how could I?). Or our little granddaughter insists on holding the saltshaker and sprinkling it over her plate by herself. Most days, I rarely experience uninterrupted thoughts, let alone moments of peaceful stillness.

But what if being still is more than just resting our bodies? Because in life, ongoing physical stillness is not usually possible. What if God is inviting us instead to be still on the inside, as I believe today's verse indicates? What if, during all the hustle and bustle of each day, our hearts could be still, trusting Him and resting in His strength and faithfulness instead of stressing and striving?

As the Lord invites us to be still, He teaches us how to do that—which is a good thing, because a still heart with busy hands seems like a contradiction. It can feel impossible. But it's not. The second portion of Psalm 46:10 says, "...and know that I am God." This is an experiential knowing, a familiarity with the One who is always with us. (See Matthew 1:23.) We *know* He is God when we know His

Word, we know His character, and we know He is always, *always* with us.

As our hearts come to know God more intimately and trust and rely on Him more deeply, even on our most demanding days and in our most active caregiving moments, when our hands remain constantly busy, we can possess beautifully still hearts.

A CAREGIVER PRAYER

Lord, though most of my days are full and my breaks few and far between, I long to possess a still heart. Will You please help me to know You more intimately and believe more firmly that You are with me, regardless of how busy I am? Help me cultivate a still heart, knowing that You love me with an everlasting love and that You are my ever-present help in times of need.

However many tasks I face each day, help me to rest in the fact that You are God. You are sovereign. You are able. You are with me. Help me to trust You and allow my heart to bask in Your goodness. Help me— every day—to be still and know that You are God. In Jesus's name, amen.

THOUGHTS FOR TODAY

+ God is inviting me to be still on the inside, through knowing Him.

+ I know God through knowing Scripture and knowing more of His character.

+ Though my hands are busy, my heart can be still.

MY THOUGHTS AND PRAYERS

DAY TWENTY-NINE
BRING THE JOY

Bring joy to your servant's life, because I appeal to you, Lord.
—Psalm 86:4

In the midst of our three geographic moves within just four years, stress truly took its toll on me. Moving several states away with our daughter and her eleven-week-old baby, adjusting to a new location and a completely different climate, felt overwhelming. I can be serious and intense by nature, but during this period of change and adjustment, I sensed that I needed to start praying for laughter. I needed joy! I actually wrote "daily laughter" on my prayer list. And I prayed earnestly.

During that season, my heart throbbed. Winter was closing in, COVID-19 was in full swing, and, oh, how I missed our friends back home. I missed my normal life! But the Lord heard my unceasing prayers, and, to my delighted surprise (and immense gratitude), I began to laugh again. Sometimes my husband and I would crack up over silly jokes. Sometimes the baby made us laugh. Sometimes Keith and I would crank up the music and cut a rug. Usually, the dog joined in, and we'd double over.

If *"a joyful heart is good medicine"* (Proverbs 17:22), then caregivers probably need a double dose—with unlimited refills. When we miss our everyday life, we feel overwhelmed, or our days become a bit too intense, a dose of daily laughter is good for our souls.

Laughter is a gift from God. It lightens our load. It exercises our insides. It reduces stress and triggers the release of dopamine, the "feel-good" hormone. It also brings balance to what can be an otherwise intense, serious time. Another place in Scripture, we're admonished, *"Don't be dejected and sad, for the joy of the LORD is your strength!"* (Nehemiah 8:10 NLT). His joy *is* our strength, and, oh, how we need it! Caregiving can feel arduous and heavy. Sometimes we need our loads lightened. Daily laughter, and the joy it produces, goes a long way toward easing the stress that accumulates.

We can appeal to the Lord for joy in our lives, as today's verse reminds us. Go ahead and ask Him for daily laughter. God will hear those prayers, and soon, laughter, which is such good medicine, will bubble out of your heart.

A CAREGIVER PRAYER

Lord, when the stress of caregiving takes its toll on me and my heart aches and is overwhelmed, help me remember to appeal to You for joy and to ask You for a daily dose of laughter. Please bring little bursts of laughter into my life throughout each day. May genuine laughter bubble out of me and cheer my soul, and even touch the loved one I am caring for.

Thank You for the gift of laughter. Thank You for using it in my life now to lighten my load and balance out what sometimes feels like such an intense and serious time. May Your grace continue to be sufficient for me and Your joy continue to be my strength. In Jesus's name, amen.

THOUGHTS FOR TODAY

+ If a joyful heart is good medicine, then caregivers need a double dose.
+ Laughter is a gift from God that lightens my load and reduces stress.
+ I can appeal to the Lord, asking Him for joy and a daily dose of laughter.

MY THOUGHTS AND PRAYERS

_____

_____

_____

_____

_____

_____

DAY THIRTY
CHOOSE TO REJOICE EVEN THOUGH

Rejoice in the Lord always. I will say it again: Rejoice!
—Philippians 4:4

Some people are a pleasure to be around. Though not perfect, they are upbeat, smile often, and have a genuinely happy outlook on life. My youngest brother, John, is one of those people. While visiting him and my sister-in-law at their home several years ago, I was pitching in and cooking dinner. About that time, John breezed through the back door after a long day of work, a wide smile on his face. He walked right over and gave me a big hug, and we talked for a few moments while I stood at the stove. Then John went on his merry way. Though brief, our encounter lifted my heart.

Of course, we're all born with different temperaments and personalities. But the key for all of us, and the primary reason behind John's joyful countenance, is that he knows, loves, and lives to serve Jesus. He truly rejoices in the Lord. He chooses to do this—every day.

Although my personality is different from my brother's, I, too, can choose to rejoice in the Lord. This is something I need to remember and do, often, especially when life is hard. Especially when things don't turn out the way I prefer.

The good news is that our lives don't have to be perfect for us to rejoice. If that were the case, there would be mighty little rejoicing happening in our homes. Instead, we're told to rejoice *in the Lord.* This means:

We can rejoice even though we're in a trying season of caregiving.

We can rejoice even though our lives might not seem fair right now.

We can rejoice even though by day's end we're depleted.

We can rejoice because the object and focus of our rejoicing is not our circumstances but our Lord. Jesus is the reason we rejoice. He is our solid Rock and our fortress. (See Psalm 18:2.) He is our ever-present help in trouble. (See Psalm 46:1.) He loves us with an everlasting love. (See Jeremiah 31:3.) And He is the focus of our rejoicing.

Just like the day my brother arrived home and greeted me so warmly, as we make the choice to rejoice in the Lord daily, Jesus will be honored, we'll be a beautiful example to our loved one, and our hearts will be lifted.

A CAREGIVER PRAYER

Lord, I need to rejoice in You. Every day. Even though my life is far from perfect. Even though I'm currently experiencing such a hard season. Even though I may not always like the way things have turned out. Will You please help me to rejoice anyway, keeping You as the object and focus of my rejoicing?

Thank You, Jesus, for being my ever-present help, my strength, my hope, and the One who lifts and restores my soul. Help me to remember to rejoice in You daily. As I do, I pray You will be honored, I will be a beautiful example to my loved one, and my heart will be encouraged. In Jesus's name, amen.

THOUGHTS FOR TODAY

+ I can choose to rejoice in the Lord daily.

+ I can rejoice even if life doesn't seem fair.

+ The object of my rejoicing is not my circumstances but Jesus.

MY THOUGHTS AND PRAYERS

_____

_____

_____

_____

_____

DAY THIRTY-ONE
TELL GOD EVERYTHING

I pour out my complaints before him
and tell him all my troubles.
—Psalm 142:2 NLT

I have probably filled God's ear more than the average human. When circumstances crush me, irk me, or cause my heart to flutter with worry, I'm a huge believer in running to God and running it all past Him. I cry out to Him, day or night, whenever the need appears. Then, right before bed, I am fond of kneeling and lifting every last concern to Him. In detail. Because it's hard to sleep when burdens are strapped across our back.

I'm in good company. King David vented to the Lord frequently and in detail. In fact, it's through reading the Psalms that I learned it's okay to vent to the Lord. It's okay to process our emotions and complaints with Him and to tell Him, in whatever level of detail our heart desires, all of our troubles. The truth is, God knows everything that concerns us anyway. It's a huge relief to tell Him not only what is happening but also how it's affecting us personally.

This is how, as caregivers, we do our part to prevent ourselves from being overcome by all the worrisome details, the issues over which we have no control, and the daily toll that caregiving takes on us.

If you struggle with thinking that your prayers are an imposition on God, or that you shouldn't bother Him because you've somehow reached the top of some arbitrary daily prayer quota, I promise you, God looks forward to your prayers. He always listens. And you are utterly free to lift your heart and your voice to Him each time that holy desire arises within you.

Proverbs 15:8 encourages us that *"the prayer of the upright is his delight."* How amazing and wonderful that our prayers delight God.

He is our good heavenly Father, and it is His joy to engage with us. And because of Jesus and the finished work of the cross, it is our privilege, as His sons and daughters, to run to Him and pour out our hearts in prayer.

A CAREGIVER PRAYER

Lord, when circumstances crush me, irk me, or make my heart flutter with worry, help me to run straight to You and to tell You, in all honesty, all of my troubles. May I never think that I am imposing on You or that I'm taking up too much of Your time. Instead, help me to recognize that You look forward to my prayers and You always listen.

I'm grateful that because of the finished work of the cross, it is my privilege, as Your precious child, to pray. Thank You that I can run to You and vent every complaint, tell You all my troubles, and pour out my heart in honest prayer to You. Thank You for deeply encouraging me as only You can. In Jesus's name, amen.

THOUGHTS FOR TODAY

+ King David vented to the Lord frequently and in detail.

+ It's okay to process my emotions and complaints to God and tell Him my troubles.

+ My prayers delight God.

MY THOUGHTS AND PRAYERS

_____

_____

_____

_____

_____

DAY THIRTY-TWO
HE SATISFIES OUR SOULS

Satisfy us in the morning with your faithful love so that we may
shout with joy and be glad all our days.
—Psalm 90:14

How very differently our days might go if, when we began to sense discouragement and heaviness in our hearts, we would cry out to God as Moses did in the Psalm above. After forty years spent traipsing through the desert with God's people in tow, he knew a thing or two about what a soul needs under harsh, unremitting circumstances.

As we work diligently at the ongoing task of caregiving, discouragement can set in. The day-to-day reality of helping our loved one and the frequent necessity of putting our own needs on the back burner can negatively impact us. There will be days when we don't feel like we can keep going. There will be days when the thought of persevering is as appealing as a cup of gray water. And there will be days when we're tempted to flat out quit.

Moses understood the remarkable soul boost that God's faithful love provides in hard circumstances. He understood the deep satisfaction we desperately need to manage well for the long haul, and he knew it could only come from almighty God. He alone can make our hearts shout with joy and be glad all our days. Not just some of our days, but all of them. Even when we're having one of *those* days.

We can begin the holy habit of praying this particular passage of Scripture each morning, crying out to the Lord and trusting Him to encourage our hearts with divine satisfaction every day. When I think about this, I picture the pleasure and satisfaction of a good home-cooked pot roast—one that simmers on the stove for hours, its mouthwatering aroma filling my home. After dinner, my stomach is satisfied. I am grateful for such a wholesome and delicious meal. In the same way, the Lord satisfies our souls.

Although our current caregiving circumstances may not necessarily be a source of continuous joy, God's faithful love is. His love never fails. His love buoys our sometimes-sinking hearts, encouraging us and filling us with supernatural joy. It's His unfailing love that deeply satisfies us, makes us glad, and equips us to serve our loved one joyfully.

A CAREGIVER PRAYER

Lord, when I begin to sense heaviness and discouragement in the difficult, day-to-day reality of caregiving, and especially when I doubt my capacity to persevere and I'm tempted to give up and quit, will You please prompt me by Your Spirit to read and pray Psalm 90:14? I don't have what it takes, Lord, but You do. Help me remember this and encourage myself with the beautiful truth of Your Word.

Satisfy me as only You can, and make me glad. Thank You for Your unfailing love, which makes me glad all of my days—not just some of them but all of them. May Your unfailing love lift my heart and fill me with the deep soul satisfaction I need to serve my loved one joyfully. In Jesus's name, amen.

THOUGHTS FOR TODAY

+ God's faithful love provides a remarkable soul boost, equipping and enabling me.

+ I desperately need God's faithful love to satisfy my soul as I serve.

+ I will begin the holy habit of praying Psalm 90:14 aloud each morning.

MY THOUGHTS AND PRAYERS

_____

_____

_____

_____

_____

_____

DAY THIRTY-THREE
HIS POWER, NOT OURS

His divine power has given us everything required for life and
godliness through the knowledge of him who called us by his
own glory and goodness.
—2 Peter 1:3

How feeble our efforts in life, and certainly in our caregiving journey. The truth is, I do not possess the capacity to meet this colossal need, and neither do you.

About two years into taking care of our then-baby granddaughter, overwhelmed by all that I was attempting to manage (and probably not doing a very good job, in spite of my efforts), I knelt beside my bed in prayer. That night, frazzled and overwhelmed, I bowed my head to ask the Lord for His help. Almost immediately, today's verse popped into my mind. I had memorized the verse, and so, as I knelt, I recited the entire thing—and felt so convicted. Over and over, the words *"His power has given us everything required for life"* came out of my mouth.

And, of course, the Lord was right. The frustration and exhaustion I experienced were natural, to a degree, given my age and the circumstances; but what I sensed the Lord pointing out to me that night brought instant clarity. I was attempting to take care of our precious granddaughter to a great degree in my own strength. God graciously gave me this friendly reminder so that I would consciously choose to rely on His divine power instead of on my own. I climbed into bed that night with tears of relief in my eyes.

When we experience an enormous sense of inadequacy in meeting any task that seems impossible (and caregiving often distinctly feels this way), it is His divine power that we need. We don't need to try harder, knuckle down, and power through. We certainly cannot manufacture the strength necessary, nor the compassion, nor the stamina that caregiving requires. It's His divine power that provides all we need.

The One who calls us by His glory and goodness has also called us to this ambitious, seemingly impossible task of caring for our loved one—for however long. I hope that, tonight, as you kneel by your bed, God reminds you, as He did me, that His divine power has given us everything required for life.

A CAREGIVER PRAYER

Lord, my efforts are so feeble. I humbly confess that I do not possess the power, compassion, or stamina this caregiving task requires. I have surrendered to this assignment and accept it, but I cannot do it in my power. Please help me not to attempt it without Your strength undergirding me.

Though I frequently feel inadequate for the task, Your power has no limitations. Your divine power strengthens, encourages, and enables me. When I feel frustrated and overwhelmed, help me gauge whether I am attempting this within my strength, and then help me to consciously rely on Yours instead. Thank You for Your divine power, which has given me everything required for life. In Jesus's name, amen.

THOUGHTS FOR TODAY

+ I do not possess the capacity to meet this colossal caregiving need alone.

+ I will ask God if I am attempting to care for my loved one in my own strength.

+ His divine power has given me everything required for life (and caregiving).

MY THOUGHTS AND PRAYERS

_____

_____

_____

_____

_____

_____

DAY THIRTY-FOUR
REMAIN FIRMLY ATTACHED

Yes, I am the vine; you are the branches.
Those who remain in me, and I in them, will produce much
fruit. For apart from me you can do nothing.
—John 15:5 NLT

A beautiful maple tree stands in our small backyard. Every fall, it is my delight to gaze at its lovely leaves shimmering in the sunny breeze, transforming from green to gold to a spectacular shade of scarlet. This year, however, 80 mph winds ripped most of the still-green leaves from the tree several weeks before autumn. Of the few leaves that remain, most are already curled and brown. Many small brown branches dangle precariously from large limbs. Though still attached to the maple tree, they are ripped beyond repair and already dead. I'm quite sad that the typically beautiful autumn foliage won't be on full display this year.

The dangling branches on our maple tree remind me of Jesus's illustration, above. If you've ever visited a vineyard, you've seen that individual grape clusters grow on small branches that hang beneath a thick, solid primary vine. As long as the branches remain firmly attached to a healthy primary vine, they'll produce grapes. In a spiritual context, we as caregivers must likewise remain firmly attached to our Lord, in utter dependence on Him for all our needs. This is how we thrive, bearing the fruit of patience, kindness, and joy, while we help our loved one through whatever the crisis demands. It's the only way.

Jesus then declared that apart from Him, we truly cannot manage. Raise your hand if you've learned this the hard way (my hand is certainly raised). He was intentionally spotlighting our inability to be fruitful without His help. When we unintentionally forget to depend on Him, or when we in our stubbornness persist in attempting the job without His help, we discover that our efforts, like dangling, shriveled branches, will not produce good fruit.

Jesus is our primary source—the true Vine—the One who infuses the richness and fullness of His Spirit into us, thereby strengthening and enabling us. As we choose to remain in Him, utterly dependent on Him, through reading Scripture and through a steady stream of prayer, our beautiful foliage will be on full display. And we will produce fruit that truly pleases, honors, and glorifies God, as well as blesses our loved one.

A CAREGIVER PRAYER

Lord, I don't want to be a dried-up, dangling branch, barely hanging on to You, the Vine. As a branch of the Lord, I recognize I am Your servant, here to accomplish Your will as I care for my loved one, but I cannot manage well apart from You.

Please help me to thrive, firmly attached to You and remaining in You—through reading Your Word and praying—throughout my day. Lord, I confess that I am utterly dependent on You. Nourish and infuse me with the rich fullness of Your Holy Spirit, enabling and equipping me as I serve. May I produce fruit that pleases, honors, and glorifies You and that blesses my loved one. In Jesus's name, amen.

THOUGHTS FOR TODAY

+ Apart from Christ, I cannot manage or serve my loved one well.

+ I must, through Scripture and prayer, remain firmly attached to my Lord.

+ Jesus—the Vine—nourishes me and infuses the richness and fullness of His Spirit into me, enabling and equipping me.

MY THOUGHTS AND PRAYERS

_____

_____

_____

_____

_____

_____

DAY THIRTY-FIVE
HOLY REMINDERS IN THE NIGHT

I will both lie down and sleep in peace, for you alone,
Lord, make me live in safety.
—Psalm 4:8

Have you ever awakened in the middle of the night, your mind inundated with many scenarios over which you're legitimately concerned, which in turn amps your body, making sleep a faraway, futile longing? If so, I understand. My body often reacts to stress in this highly inconvenient and frankly annoying manner.

When, on occasion, my eyes pop open for no apparent reason other than stress related to current circumstances, sometimes I will lie in bed and pray. However, surprisingly, sometimes that backfires, as it causes me to micro-focus on unpleasant, nerve-racking details, which is anything but relaxing. Don't get me wrong—I do still pray in the middle of the night when prompted by the Spirit. However, I have learned to discern when I should pray and when I should counsel my own heart, filling it up with truth and encouragement.

Sometimes, what our hearts and minds most need in the middle of the night are holy reminders. Reminders of God's faithfulness. Of His nearness. Of His goodness. Reminders that He is with us in the fire and that we don't have to be afraid. Reminders that we are not alone and that, ultimately, God is sovereign and firmly in control.

One of the many benefits of memorizing Scripture is the calming, reassuring effect God's Word has on our souls. The habit of hiding God's Word in my heart (see Psalm 119:11) has been life-changing for me, especially in the middle of the night.

Now, when I wake up at three in the morning, instead of hyper-focusing on the problem, hardship, or crisis du jour, I scroll through my memory bank and declare truth to myself. One of my favorite go-to verses that I submit for your memorization consideration is today's verse: "*I will both lie down and sleep in peace, for you alone,* Lord, *make me live in safety*" (Psalm 4:8).

I need to hear myself say these words repeatedly. My guess is that you may also benefit from speaking them. God's Word reassures us, calms us, encourages us, and reminds us of what is true. In the dark of night, when situations are magnified and hope teeters, declaring Scripture strengthens our hearts and helps our faith grow.

A CAREGIVER PRAYER

Lord, when I wake up in the middle of the night due to stress, give me the discernment to know if I should pray or if I should counsel my heart with Your Word (or both!). When my heart and mind need a holy reminder, help me to recall the verses I have hidden in my heart and use them to comfort and calm my mind and body.

Thank You, Lord, that Your Word reassures me, calms me, encourages me, and reminds me of what is true. Thank You for reminding me, in the middle of the night, that You are with me, that You are faithful, and that You are sovereign. May my heart and body then completely rest in Your awesome peace. In Jesus's name, amen.

THOUGHTS FOR TODAY

- Sometimes, what my heart and mind most need in the middle of the night are holy reminders.

- Instead of hyper-focusing on the problem, hardship, or crisis du jour, I can focus on a verse of Scripture.

- God's Word reassures me, calms me, encourages me, and reminds me of what is true.

MY THOUGHTS AND PRAYERS

_____

_____

_____

_____

_____

_____

TRUST HIM AND SOAR

But those who trust in the LORD will renew their strength; they
will soar on wings like eagles; they will run and not become
weary, they will walk and not faint.
—Isaiah 40:31

On a scale of one to ten, with one being the lowest and ten being the highest, where would you gauge your trust level in the Lord? Is it easy for you to trust God in harsh or unexpected conditions, or are your typical responses more along the range of backing away, doubting, or attempting to manipulate and/or control the situation?

It is hard to walk through horrible, shocking, or heartbreaking circumstances. Trusting God when facing a major life upheaval—such as shifting around our schedules and our very lives to care for a loved one—is not easy, nor does it come naturally to many of us. And trusting God when the outcome is uncertain (hello, that's essentially all of life!) is probably hardest of all.

But the reality is that we don't have to know all the details before we trust Him. We don't have to know how long this will last before we trust Him. We certainly don't have to know all the answers or the outcome before we trust Him. *"For we walk by faith, not by sight"* (2 Corinthians 5:7). This means we trust Him not because we know how everything is going to work out but because we don't. By faith, we can choose to trust God, which becomes easier as we focus more on Him and get to know Him more intimately.

The key to trusting God more is knowing Him more, becoming more familiar with His character. For instance, Psalm 145:8 says, *"The LORD is gracious and compassionate, slow to anger and great in faithful love."* This verse reveals God's patient, tender, faithfully loving nature toward us. Knowing truths like these reassures us and helps us to trust Him in all things.

Trusting God brings great reward. It actually renews our strength, and isn't that what we desperately need? Trusting the Lord enables us to soar and run as we focus on the work at hand, helping our loved one, without growing spiritually discouraged and faint. As we decide to trust the Lord, we can run without becoming weary; we can soar, spiritually speaking, because the Lord Himself refreshes and revives us.

A CAREGIVER'S PRAYER

Lord, I confess that trusting You completely is not always easy, but I am willing to take steps to change that. Will You please give me grace and time to know You more? Give me a hunger for Your Word, and, as I read my Bible, reveal Yourself to me. Help me gain a deeper understanding of Your character, which will enable me to trust You more fully.

I'm grateful that as I trust You, I am strengthened. May my ability to trust You increase, and may my strength increase. As I care for my loved one, may I soar on wings like eagles. May I run and not grow weary. May I walk and not faint. In Jesus's name, amen.

THOUGHTS FOR TODAY

+ I don't have to have all the details or know all the answers before I trust God.

+ I can choose to walk by faith and not by sight.

+ I can trust God more by knowing Him more, through reading His Word.

MY THOUGHTS AND PRAYERS

_____

_____

_____

_____

_____

DAY THIRTY-SEVEN
A CONTENTED HEART

But godliness with contentment is great gain.
—1 Timothy 6:6

To be honest, finding my footing after becoming a caregiver for our newborn granddaughter was challenging. And she was adorable! Initially, I attempted to juggle my writing ministry, continue leading a Bible study, fulfill church commitments, manage housework and laundry, and do all the other things. Of necessity, and because I don't multitask well, I made the prayerful decision to back-burner my writing. Although writing articles and books was a ministry the Lord had placed me in, I realized that this unexpected ministry of helping our daughter and caring for her newborn trumped everything else. And it was (and still is) a valuable, important ministry.

I have never regretted that decision. Although it has been fraught with strain and exhaustion, I have always known it was the right choice. But that doesn't mean I didn't struggle. I did. Finding contentment in this new place has proven tough—a sometimes-daily choice.

Perhaps the following list of my many struggles might match some of yours as you walk out your commitment as a caregiver. I have wrestled with resentment, discouragement, isolation, fear, anxiety, sleeplessness, grief, the stress of balancing it all, and depression. Many of these surprised me. After all, I saw an undeniable need, and meeting that need was clearly the right choice. However, reality hits hard when life shifts and the change is sudden and dramatic.

As I wrestled my way through that ugly, lengthy list, the Lord consistently brought me back to today's verse. Yes, these were supposed to be the golden years for my husband and me. *"Godliness with contentment is great gain."* No, my house is not spick-and-span anymore. *"Godliness with contentment is great gain."* Yes, my heart can sometimes feel overwhelmed. *"Godliness with contentment is great gain."* No, I was unable to continue leading a Bible study. *"Godliness with contentment is great gain."* Whatever your current caregiving role and its challenges, know this: the work you're engaged in is valuable and meaningful.

Through it all, I have learned (and continue to learn) the exceeding value of a contented heart. Trusting that God has placed me here is paramount. Surrendering to this season and accepting it brings peace. Every assignment has a blessing woven into it, and as we enjoy our granddaughter to a degree we might not have otherwise, my hope is that God will show you the blessing in your role, as well, and grant you a contented heart.

A CAREGIVER'S PRAYER

Lord, You know the list of issues I have struggled with since becoming a caregiver. Though reality has hit hard, and my life has shifted (for now), I choose to trust You. I choose to surrender afresh and to accept this place where You have brought me.

Help me to remember that the work I am engaged in is valuable and important because my loved one is important to You and to me. As I walk through this caregiving commitment, weave in a blessing and help me to see and appreciate it. Help me to choose to remember that godliness with contentment is great gain. In Jesus's name, amen.

THOUGHTS FOR TODAY

+ Finding contentment in my role as caregiver is sometimes a daily choice.
+ The work I'm engaged in is valuable and important.
+ Surrendering to and accepting my current assignment brings peace and contentment.

MY THOUGHTS AND PRAYERS

_____

_____

_____

_____

_____

_____

DAY THIRTY-EIGHT
AVOIDING THE COMPARISON TRAP

Let each person examine his own work,
and then he can take pride in himself alone, and not compare
himself with someone else.
—Galatians 6:4

Because our lives look radically different when we choose to obey God by helping our loved one, we can sometimes fall into the comparison trap. And sometimes we don't even realize that's what's happening.

For instance, a year ago, my husband and I attended a holiday dinner party at our neighbor's home. A jolly Christmas wreath glittered as we rang the doorbell. But I could hardly have imagined the extent of the lovely, festive, perfectly decorated holiday cheer that awaited us. Their pristine home gleamed. Multiple charming, twinkling little Christmas trees sat cozily in various nooks. Bookshelves and side tables were adorned with cheerful, sparkling vignettes. Even the walls glowed with truly lovely, fragrant decorations. Loveliest of all was the dining table, featuring classic, breathtaking centerpieces and an eclectic array of mismatched, yet all beautiful, silver, gold, and cream-colored tableware.

Hours later, after a sumptuous meal, a fun time playing games, and lots of flowing conversation, my husband and I landed with a thud in our own sparsely decorated, not spotless home across the street. The truth was, I hadn't found the energy or desire to decorate much that year, and that was okay. However, the feelings lurking in my heart were definitely not. Suddenly, all the pretty yet simple and sparse decorations I had lovingly set out seemed inadequate.

Thankfully, when we do recognize, through the Spirit's nudge, that we're falling into the comparison trap, we will hopefully remember that *"godliness with contentment is great gain"* (1 Timothy 6:6).

When, by God's grace, we are convicted, we can bow our hearts and begin adjusting our attitudes. And we can choose to be grateful for the many blessings we still possess, allowing ourselves to be content in our current season.

It's okay to acknowledge that our lives are currently different from our peers'. Our days don't look the same. Our homes may not look the same. Our priorities are definitely not the same. I didn't (and still don't) have the free time my sweet neighbor enjoys. Maybe one day I will. Maybe one day you will, too. However, right now, we must focus on the task at hand, cultivate gratitude, and resist the temptation to fall into the comparison trap.

A CAREGIVER'S PRAYER

Lord, it's true that my life looks radically different in this current caregiving season. Will You please help me not to compare my life and all my daily living constraints with those of friends, family, and neighbors? If and when I begin to fall into the comparison trap, please convict me and help me adjust my attitude to be grateful for the many blessings I possess.

Help me to focus on the task at hand, and fill me with Your peace and joy as I do the work that You have called me to do. Help me, by Your grace, to be content with my current situation and to cultivate a thankful heart, today and always. In Christ's name, amen.

THOUGHTS FOR TODAY

+ When, by God's grace, I am convicted of comparison, I can bow my heart and adjust my attitude.

+ I can choose gratitude for the many blessings I do possess.

+ By God's grace, I can focus on the task at hand, choose gratitude, and refuse to fall into the comparison trap.

MY THOUGHTS AND PRAYERS

_____

_____

_____

_____

_____

_____

DAY THIRTY-NINE
A GOOD SEASON

For everything there is a season,
and a time for every matter under heaven.
—Ecclesiastes 3:1 ESV

As caregivers, it is essential that we regularly remind ourselves that we are currently living in a season designated and orchestrated by almighty God. It's not necessarily an easy season, and perhaps it was not one we anticipated, but, as the verse above assures us, it is a season God has ordained—for us and our loved one. In this season of pouring ourselves out for the benefit of another, we will face trials and discouragement. We will encounter hardships, unpleasant circumstances, and difficult issues that can sometimes cloud the big picture of all we're doing and prevent us from viewing this season accurately.

But what if, instead of considering the time we spend assisting our loved one as an obligation, a sentence, or a mandatory, hard season akin to time in Siberia, we asked God to adjust our perspective? And what if, through that request, we could not only embrace this demanding season, but even enjoy it? Particularly when we're in it for the long haul, I believe this is a request every one of us should make of the Lord.

When we allow God to transform our hearts and shift our perspective, everything changes. We begin seeing things differently. Our caregiving season can then become:

A season of joy.

A season of peace.

A season of spiritual growth.

A season of tremendous blessing.

A season of knowing God more intimately.

A season of more earnest prayer.

A season of deep satisfaction.

Not only can the Lord make our current season a greater blessing to us personally, but we can also grow in fruitfulness and faith. God uses every season we are in *"to work together for the good of those who love God and are called according to his purpose for them"* (Romans 8:28 NLT).

As I look back over the years my husband and I have spent helping our daughter by caring for our granddaughter, I praise God for shifting my perspective. It has saved me untold bitterness and transformed the way I see and experience my current assignment. In this time under heaven, may each of us experience a greater capacity for joy, peace, spiritual growth, blessing, knowing God, praying earnestly, and deep satisfaction. May this season under heaven be a good season.

A CAREGIVER'S PRAYER

Lord, I trust that I am living in a season designed and completely orchestrated by You, but I'm not entirely sure that I always view this time accurately. Will You please shift my perspective and help me to see this time the way You do? Give me a fresh, divine perspective so I won't view it negatively and can instead embrace and enjoy this season.

Help me to allow You to transform my heart and completely change my perspective so that I see things differently. In this current time under heaven, may I, by Your grace, experience a greater capacity for joy, peace, spiritual growth, blessing, intimacy with You, earnest prayer, and deep satisfaction. May this season under heaven be a good one. In Christ's name, amen.

THOUGHTS FOR TODAY

+ I am currently living in a season designed and orchestrated by almighty God.

+ I can better embrace and enjoy this season when I ask God to adjust my perspective.

+ God enables me to experience joy, peace, spiritual growth, blessing, intimacy with Him, earnest prayer, and deep satisfaction in my caregiving season.

MY THOUGHTS AND PRAYERS

_____

_____

_____

_____

_____

_____

DAY FORTY
FEAR NOT

I sought the LORD, and he answered me
and delivered me from all my fears.
—Psalm 34:4 ESV

Which fear has the strongest grip on your heart right now? My caregiving experience started poorly because of fear, which took up a larger portion of my days (and nights) than I would have liked. My fear was debilitating, even affecting me physically, and though I partly understood the reason behind it, I had a hard time battling it. A significant portion of my fear was based on reality. But the rest of the fear I experienced was thanks to my uncanny, remarkable ability to play out worst-case scenarios in my mind. This is just a fancy name for worrying. Not exactly a handy gift, unless you're an author of horror stories.

Though a substantial learning curve was involved, I eventually recognized fear's relentless attacks and remembered that I wasn't helpless. And neither are you. The truth is that when fear bombards us, we aren't powerless. We don't have to continue to put up with the likes of cold, dark fear gripping our hearts. Whether fear manifests as panic, anxiety, worry, or our waking up afraid in the middle of the night, our ammunition in this battle is mightier than every lie our minds manufacture and stronger than fear itself. This weapon? God's Word.

We combat the lie of fear by hiding specific biblical truths in our hearts. Write them on sticky notes, enter them on your phone, or print them out on a 3 x 5 card. Every time fear strikes, allow God's Word to embed itself snugly into your heart. Truth is greater than fear, and it wins every time. Here are just a few specific verses you can run to when fear hits hard:

When you're flat out afraid:

"Do not fear, for I am with you; do not be afraid, for I am your God. I will strengthen you; I will help you; I will hold on to you with my righteous right hand" (Isaiah 41:10).

When your mind makes up worst-case scenarios:

"Don't worry about anything, but in everything, through prayer and petition with thanksgiving, present your requests to God" (Philippians 4:6).

When you're afraid that you're unable to keep going, you feel weak, or you want to quit:

"Finally, be strengthened by the Lord and by his vast strength" (Ephesians 6:10).

When we feel troubled and frightened, we must run to the Lord, pouring out our hearts in all honesty and crying out for His help. We must use the weapon of His Word, which is truth. And He, in His great power and faithfulness, will deliver us from all our fears.

A CAREGIVER'S PRAYER
Lord, You know the fear that I battle and the hold it sometimes has on my heart. God, I cry out to You for deliverance and complete freedom from debilitating fear. Enable me to be strong, bold, and very courageous. When fear bombards me, help me to remember that I am not powerless. Give me great grace to hide Your Word in my heart and use it as ammunition against fear's attacks every single time it hits hard.

Thank You, Lord, that when I'm afraid, I can trust in You. You are faithful, You are mighty, and You are greater than all my fears. Your Word, which is truth, puts fear in its place. Thank You that as I seek You, You answer me and deliver me from all my fears. In Christ's name, amen.

THOUGHTS FOR TODAY
+ The truth is that when fear bombards me, I am not powerless.

+ I combat the lie of fear by hiding specific biblical truths in my heart.

♦ When I cry out to the Lord, He, in His great power and faithfulness, will deliver me from all my fears.

MY THOUGHTS AND PRAYERS

_____

_____

_____

_____

_____

_____

DAY FORTY-ONE
YOU ARE MORE THAN A CONQUEROR

Yet amid all these things we are more than conquerors and gain
a surpassing victory through Him Who loved us.
—Romans 8:37 AMPC

Reading nonfiction books written by or about those who have overcome extremely hard, seemingly impossible circumstances is a favorite personal hobby. One of my favorite books features the backstories of popular hymns. Spotlighting personal hardships, abysmal life circumstances, and dire situations, this book proves that many well-known hymns were born out of difficulty. Hundreds of years later, these hymns are still sung worldwide, all because someone followed God's plan, trusted Him, and chose to be obedient, in spite of great personal cost.

Guess what? As a caregiver, you, too, are currently walking out hard circumstances. You, too, are following God's plan, trusting Him, and choosing to be obedient, sometimes in spite of great personal cost. As we honor God with our lives in this season by caring for our loved one, that person is blessed, and God is glorified. Though we may not write a book or a hymn about it, God is using all these things to make us more than conquerors. Today's verse also reminds us that as we trust and honor and obey the Lord, we *"gain a surpassing victory through Him Who loved us"*—that's Jesus!

As the verse above declares, *"amid all these things we are more than conquerors."* And so it is for us as caregivers. Amid pressure, concerns, physical fatigue, and exhaustion, even when it doesn't feel like it could possibly be an accurate depiction of ourselves as believers walking out God's will and plans for us, we are indeed more than conquerors. Our surpassing victory occurs when we choose to trust God in hardship, remain faithful to the task He has called us to, and persevere for however long it takes.

Perhaps no one except you, your loved one, and a few family members will ever know of or acknowledge your sacrifice this side of eternity. My friend, take heart. The Lord sees your hard work. He knows of your faithfulness and is aware of your endurance. And in His eyes, by His effusive grace, you are much more than a conqueror.

A CAREGIVER'S PRAYER

Lord, I am Your servant, come to do Your will. By Your grace, I will continue to care for my loved one and persevere for however long it takes, trusting You every step of the way. Lord, as I struggle through pressures, concerns, and exhaustion, strengthen my weary body and fill my heart and mind with gladness and gratitude.

As I walk out Your plan for me in this season, please develop my character so that I truly am more than a conqueror. Help me to trust You and love well. Encourage and strengthen me and help me to keep my eyes on Jesus, by whom I gain a surpassing victory. In Christ's name, amen.

THOUGHTS FOR TODAY

+ I am following God's plan, trusting Him, and choosing to be obedient.

+ As I trust and honor and obey the Lord, I gain a surpassing victory through Him who loved us (Jesus).

+ As a believer walking out God's will and plans for me, I am more than a conqueror.

MY THOUGHTS AND PRAYERS

_____

_____

_____

_____

_____

DAY FORTY-TWO
HE STEADIES OUR SHAKY HEARTS

When the earth and all its inhabitants shake,
I am the one who steadies its pillars.
—Psalm 75:3

This is a big promise from an even bigger God. When we observe the state of our country and world, our natural human tendency is to quake with uncertainty and even fear. As caregivers, we can experience a similar response when our little worlds shake. Back when my caregiving journey started, I recall wondering if my life would ever be normal again. Nothing felt the same because, in truth, my ordinary life had drastically shifted. And, of course, there were ripple effects that touched nearly every area of my life.

How grateful I am that when everything around me is shaking, God is the stabilizing force I desperately need. When our everyday lives collide with the reality of watching over and caring for our loved one, everything can feel askew. The rhythm of our life shifts, and it can be hard to gain our footing. Yet in the verse above, the Lord reminds us that He is the one who steadies the pillars of not only the earth but also our tottering hearts. When everything around us wobbles, He is our Rock and our Refuge.

Apart from the Lord, it's not possible to gain our bearings. Our hearts and emotions are unreliable gauges that we cannot always depend on. But our mighty God, who is aware of our current situation and deeply loves and cares for us, is trustworthy and dependable. He is the One who stabilizes us. He is the One who calms us. He is the One who enables us to be flexible beyond what we ever imagined. He is the One who steadies us.

Through His power and grace, we regain our bearings. In the midst of our legitimate wobble-inducing concerns, He helps us adjust course and remain steady. A verse in a favorite hymn says, "A mighty fortress is our God, a bulwark never failing."[2] A bulwark is a wall of defense. God will faithfully steady and strengthen us with the massive wall of His presence. He is indeed our mighty fortress, and His ability to stabilize us will not give way or fail. When our world shakes, we can fully rely on Him.

A CAREGIVER'S PRAYER

Lord, it seems as though almost everything in my life has shifted. My days sometimes feel shaky, and I occasionally wonder if my life will ever return to normal. While I don't have that answer, I do trust that my times are in Your hands, and I am grateful that You are the One who faithfully steadies my sometimes-wobbly heart and emotions.

Thank You, Lord, for Your deep love and care for me. You are the One who stabilizes me, calms me, and enables me to be flexible and regain my footing. Please consistently calm the pillars of my heart and emotions, for, truly, You are a bulwark that never fails, and I can fully rely on You. In Christ's name, amen.

THOUGHTS FOR TODAY

+ When everything around me is shaking, God is the stabilizing force I desperately need.

+ My heart and emotions are unreliable gauges that I cannot always depend on.

+ God is a mighty fortress; when my world shakes, I can rely on Him.

MY THOUGHTS AND PRAYERS

---

2. Martin Luther, "A Mighty Fortress," Hymnary.org, https://hymnary.org/text/a_mighty_fortress_is_our_god_a_bulwark.

DAY FORTY-THREE
RENEWED DAILY

Therefore we do not give up. Even though our outer person is
being destroyed, our inner person is being renewed day by day.
—2 Corinthians 4:16

If you've recently teetered on the edge of quitting, you're probably not alone. According to the National Alliance for Caregiving and AARP, family caregivers spend an average of 24.4 hours per week providing care. And nearly 1 in 4 caregivers spends 41 hours or more per week providing care.[3] If you fall anywhere within that range, chances are, you're tired. Possibly throw-in-the-towel tired. During the summertime and all the school breaks throughout the year, we care for our little granddaughter for over 50 hours a week. On those days, by seven o'clock in the evening, I am so depleted that I collapse into a chair, and good luck prying me out of it.

This is the reality of our frail, human bodies. We're subject to physical exhaustion and ailments. It's why Paul acknowledges that *"our outer person is being destroyed,"* and that process doesn't slow down just because we're caregivers. Though I am determined by God's grace not to quit (and I hope that is your stance, as well), I will be the first to admit that my outer person—my physical body—is being destroyed, little by little.

But that's only half of the story. Because, as this awesome verse in 2 Corinthians tells us, something remarkable, something divine, is happening at the exact same time. Our inner person is being renewed. As we determine to trust God and honor Him by fulfilling this hallowed commitment, something beautiful is happening in our hearts, because His Spirit is at work within us. While we faithfully minister to our loved one, He faithfully renews us, little by little.

---

3. Family Caregiver Alliance, "Caregiver Statistics: Demographics."

As we honor and trust Jesus in this divine assignment, taking care of all He has entrusted to us, we are, by His Spirit, being renewed day by day. This encourages us to persevere. We don't give up! This renewal also transforms our hearts and minds. It increases our endurance and fills us with hope and courage.

Next to the prayer chair in my study, I have written on a 3 x 5 card, "My inner person is being renewed day by day!" as a reminder of what's actually happening on the inside, despite what I'm well aware is happening on the outside. It's so good to know we're being renewed daily.

A CAREGIVER'S PRAYER

Lord, You are aware of the time(s) I have wanted to give up. Will You please help me to remember that this caregiving journey is a hallowed commitment, first and foremost to You, but also to one who truly needs my help? Give me grace to continue and not give up. Help me trust that as I pour myself out on their behalf, You will pour Yourself into me and renew me day by day.

As I reconcile myself to the fact that my outer person is being destroyed, thank You that at the exact same time, You are remarkably renewing me on the inside. Thank You for renewing my entire inner person and filling me with endurance, hope, and courage. In Christ's name, amen.

THOUGHTS FOR TODAY

+ I am determined by God's grace not to give up.

+ While I faithfully minister to my loved one, Jesus faithfully renews me, little by little.

+ I will remember that my inner person is being renewed day by day.

MY THOUGHTS AND PRAYERS

_____

_____

_____

_____

_____

_____

DAY FORTY-FOUR
YES, JESUS LOVES ME

I have loved you with an everlasting love; therefore,
I have continued to extend faithful love to you.
—Jeremiah 31:3

An uplifting, encouraging habit to get into while we serve as caregivers is to notice small ways the Lord encourages us each day. The ability to make our loved one smile, to remind one another of God's faithfulness, or even to sing a hymn or worship song together lightens our hearts. If your loved one cannot or will not sing, sing anyway! Singing and humming keep our hearts in tune with the Lord and encourage us as we go about each day's chores.

One of my joys in caring for our granddaughter has been teaching her hymns. Especially on days when she is especially grumpy, when she is fretful because she misses her mommy, or when she's running a fever, I drop what I'm doing, ease into my rocking chair, and have her climb onto my lap. We rock and sing together. Often, she chimes in. Sometimes she just listens. Either way, both of our hearts are calmed and cheered.

The first hymn I taught my granddaughter was "Jesus Loves Me, This I Know." She knew it before she was two years old, and, oh, what a joy it was to hear her sweet little voice singing as she played or as we drove to the grocery store. This hymn, written by Anna Bartlett Warner in 1859, is filled with priceless reminders of God's great love for us. On my most troubling days, hearing my granddaughter's tender little voice proclaiming biblical truths boosts my heart.

As we care for our loved one, a simple song and verse reminding us of God's everlasting love makes all the difference in our day. God loves us. His love for us is everlasting, based not on our most ardent efforts but on His faithfulness. God's love brings reassurance so that when the hard days come (and they always do), our hearts are reassured and comforted. His love is not temporary but eternal, based not on our efforts but on our perfect Savior's sacrifice and merit.

Let's intentionally remember that, according to today's verse, God will continue to extend His faithful love to us. It will never stop. His love for us will never grow old, and His love never fails. (See 1 Corinthians 13:8.) As you dwell on this, may your heart be encouraged. And may you be found singing (or humming), "Jesus loves me, this I know, for the Bible tells me so."[4]

A CAREGIVER'S PRAYER

Lord, help me to develop the habit of noticing the small ways You encourage me each day. Whether it is a lovely sunrise, a cardinal outside my window, or a child's cheerful song, may I notice and appreciate these small encouragements from You. May they refresh and lift my heart.

Will You please bring hymns or worship songs to my mind throughout the day to keep my heart in tune with Yours? Help me take a moment to read a psalm or a specific verse that I find especially meaningful. Thank You, Father of every good and perfect gift, for encouraging me and enabling me to go about my tasks with a merry heart, by Your great grace. In Jesus's name, amen.

THOUGHTS FOR TODAY

+ I can begin the habit of noticing small ways the Lord encourages me each day.

+ A simple song and verse reminding me of God's love makes all the difference in my day.

+ God's love for me is not temporary but eternal, based not on my efforts but on my perfect Savior's merit.

---

4. Anna Bartlett Warner, "Jesus Loves Me, This I Know," Hymnary.org, https://hymnary.org/text/jesus_loves_me_this_i_know_for_the_bible.

MY THOUGHTS AND PRAYERS

_____

_____

_____

_____

_____

_____

DAY FORTY-FIVE
OUR STRONG AND MIGHTY GOD

Finally, be strengthened by the Lord and by his vast strength.
—Ephesians 6:10

My husband and I sat on wooden pews, sunlight pouring through lovely lancet windows, as our granddaughter and her classmates filed onto the platform at the front of her school's church. Her mom, seated next to me, beamed. As the piano began playing, sweet, earnest voices filled the sanctuary with children's praises, and cute little arms lifted and made the motions that the teachers had diligently taught their students. As our granddaughter sang, "My God is so great, so strong and so mighty, there's nothing my God cannot do," her arms flexed in a muscleman pose, and I couldn't help grinning.

Oh, how I need to remember this scene when school is out and we care for our granddaughter ten hours a day, five days a week. Keith and I often tag team so that each of us can accomplish whatever that day requires without interruption (it's how I'm writing this chapter right now). Even so, neither of us has the strength required, at our age, to care for a little one for long hours. Perhaps you are nodding your head, feeling the same way in your current caregiving situation.

The truth is, none of us has the capacity to do what God is asking of us. We are frail humans with limited capacity. But our God is great and strong and mighty. There's nothing He cannot do! When the Lord strengthens us, we are supernaturally enabled to do what we never could accomplish apart from Him. God's strength is vast. He has no limitations.

The Lord is not surprised by our inadequacies; He is keenly aware of our physical, mental, emotional, and even spiritual short-comings. Thank God our deficiencies are no hindrance for Him. Our lack is more than made up for by God's abundant strength. His grace rushes in to fulfill every need—it's how we do everything.

When what we're facing far exceeds our abilities, we mustn't be surprised and we mustn't be discouraged. We must remember that our strength does not come from ourselves but from the Lord. The *Amplified Version, Classic Edition* translates today's verse in a way that brings fresh insight: *"Be strong in the Lord [be empowered through your union with Him]; draw your strength from Him [that strength which His boundless might provides]"* (Ephesians 6:10).

We are empowered by our union with Christ. We draw our strength from Him, not from ourselves. He is the one who is strong and mighty.

A CAREGIVER'S PRAYER

Lord, I don't actually have the capacity, in myself, to do all that You are asking me to do. May my acute awareness of this serve as Your way of helping me recognize my weakness. May it compel me to lean on You and trust You for more strength and grace. Though I am a frail human with limited capacity, You, God, are strong and mighty. There is nothing You cannot do!

Even though I am often surprised by my inadequacies, I'm grateful that You are keenly aware of them and that, in Your great kindness and power, Your grace rushes in and equips me with Your mighty strength. May I be continually empowered by my union with You, Lord, and may I consistently draw my strength from You. In Jesus's name, amen.

THOUGHTS FOR TODAY

+ I am a frail human with limited capacity, but my God is great, strong, and mighty.

+ God's strength is vast; He has no limitations.

+ I am empowered through my union with Christ and draw my strength from Him.

MY THOUGHTS AND PRAYERS

_____

_____

_____

_____

_____

_____

DAY FORTY-SIX
YOU ARE NEVER ALONE

And remember, I am with you always, to the end of the age.
—Matthew 28:20

What a comfort to know, deep down in our souls, that we are never alone. According to the Gospel of Matthew, these were Jesus's final words before He ascended to heaven. Jesus knew what His disciples and followers desperately needed to hear. He was leaving them for heaven, but not really, because His promised Spirit would be with all of them at once. His Spirit would not be constrained by the limitations of a human body.

Sometimes I think we would all benefit by writing today's verse on a sticky note and attaching it to our forehead. We desperately need Christ's reassuring words to take root deeply in our hearts and flourish there. That way, when the demands of our caregiving cause us to be more isolated than we'd like, we can maintain the accurate, biblical perspective that we are never alone.

Though Jesus now sits at the right hand of God the Father, His Spirit is at work mightily worldwide, in the life of every believer. According to John 15:26, the Holy Spirit is known by many names:

He is our Comforter—He understands how difficult the task is and how overwhelmed our hearts become, and He comforts and reassures us in our trials, griefs, and afflictions.

He is our Counselor—teaching and counseling us through His Word, reminding us of truths our hearts need to hear as we navigate the demands and challenges of caregiving.

He is our Helper—providing grace, wisdom, and knowledge. He leads us, guides us, and grants us insight and understanding.

He is our Advocate—supporting us, encouraging and helping us, cheering us on.

He is our Intercessor—how reassuring to know that the Holy Spirit actually prays for us! *"In the same way the Spirit also helps us in our weakness, because we do not know what to pray for as we should, but the Spirit himself intercedes for us with inexpressible groanings"* (Romans 8:26).

He is our Strengthener—He girds us with His power. He strengthens us not only physically but also mentally and emotionally. *"'Not by strength or by might, but by my Spirit,' says the LORD of Armies"* (Zechariah 4:6).

He is our Standby—He can always be relied on, ever ready to help in times of distress, emergency, or great need. We can always count on the Spirit of Jesus when we need Him.

Through His Spirit, Jesus is in fact constantly with us. By His Spirit, we are helped, strengthened, and uplifted. Praise God, it's true. We are never alone because our Savior, Redeemer, and Friend is always with us.

A CAREGIVER'S PRAYER

Lord, thank You that I am never alone. Even when I spend long, sometimes lonely, days serving my loved one, help me to encourage myself by remembering that You are always with me through Your precious Spirit.

May I consistently remember that I am reassured by the Comforter, taught by the Counselor, given knowledge and understanding by the Helper, supported and encouraged by the Advocate, prayed for by the Intercessor, girded with power by the Strengthener, and helped in distressing times by the Standby. In Jesus's name, amen.

THOUGHTS FOR TODAY

+ Even when I feel isolated or lonely, I can remember that I am not actually alone.

+ The Holy Spirit supports me as my Comforter, Counselor, Helper, Advocate, Intercessor, Strengthener, and Standby.

+ I am deeply reassured, helped, and uplifted in knowing Jesus is always with me.

MY THOUGHTS AND PRAYERS

_____

_____

_____

_____

_____

_____

DAY FORTY-SEVEN
WHO, ME? SELFISH?

Do nothing out of selfish ambition or conceit, but in humility
consider others as more important than yourselves.
—Philippians 2:3

One stark truth I've had to face repeatedly through my journey as a caregiver is my selfishness. In an internal tug-of-war, I constantly battle my selfish desires. It's embarrassing to admit how often these thoughts can pop into my mind: "I'd like my life back. I need more time for myself. I want more freedom to pursue my interests. I don't feel like battling a cantankerous toddler today. I wish my husband and I had more time together." On and on it goes.

To be honest, the level of selfishness in my own heart that has come to light over the four-plus years of caring for our granddaughter has both surprised and discouraged me. But God uses taxing, strenuous, demanding seasons to expose many things, one of which is just how selfish we can be. My guess is that caregiving requires far more than any of us ever imagined it would, and this exposes a level of personal selfishness few of us knew existed.

I'm continually amazed (and grateful) that God doesn't wash His hands of us but constantly encourages us through His Word to rise above these thoughts and above selfish living. Thankfully, *"The Lord—the Lord is a compassionate and gracious God, slow to anger and abounding in faithful love and truth"* (Exodus 34:6).

There is divine purpose happening here. Selfishness may be identified in our hearts, but it doesn't have to stay there. The Lord spotlights our selfishness to humble us, so that we will confess it and cry out to Him for forgiveness and transformation. He faithfully forgives us and changes us so that we can become more like His Son, the suffering Servant.

When our heart's desire is to honor God with our attitude and to willingly, obediently do the current task He has placed in front of us, He infuses us with immense grace. He enables us to let go of selfish ambition and serve our loved one in humility, truly considering them more important than ourselves. This response honors and pleases our Savior, who came not to be served but to serve others. (See Matthew 20:28.) And it makes us more like Him, to God's great glory.

A CAREGIVER'S PRAYER

Oh, Lord, change me! You are gracious and compassionate, slow to anger and abounding in faithful love and truth. Thank You for not giving up on me, for forgiving me as I confess my selfishness, and for transforming me so that I more accurately reflect Jesus.

Give me great grace to serve as Jesus did. Help me not to consider my life as my own but to willingly lay down my life in this way for this season that You have brought to me. Help me to do nothing out of selfish ambition or conceit but, in true humility, to consider others as better than myself. By Your immense grace, help me to be a humble, obedient servant, like Your Son. It's in His awesome name that I pray, amen.

THOUGHTS FOR TODAY

+ God uses taxing, strenuous, demanding seasons to expose my selfishness.

+ Selfishness may be identified in my heart, but it doesn't have to stay there.

+ God enables me to let go of selfish ambition and to serve my loved one in humility, truly considering them more important than myself.

MY THOUGHTS AND PRAYERS

_____

_____

_____

_____

_____

_____

DAY FORTY-EIGHT
A GENTLE SERVANT

Who among you is wise and understanding?
By his good conduct he should show that his works are done in
the gentleness that comes from wisdom.
—James 3:13

I will never forget the Tuesday morning when my then-five-year-old daughter and eleven-year-old son slid down the banister at church after women's Bible study. Not because they got hurt or injured anyone else. Not even because they caused a ruckus. But because one of the elders of the church witnessed their escapade and gently alerted me. John was so kind and tender that I scarcely understood that my children had misbehaved.

The reason I still remember the incident is that I had never been approached in such a remarkably gentle manner, especially about mischievous children doing what they knew they shouldn't. As a child, I had never been treated gently or even had things explained to me. Harsh violence had been the reality for my four younger siblings and myself growing up. But John was drastically different. And, honestly, until that moment, I didn't even know it was possible to convey an unpleasant message with such gentleness.

Today's verse tells us that wisdom from above—God's wisdom—produces good conduct, and gentleness in particular. In other words, wise people display wisdom through their behavior. Gentleness is the result of wisdom! Who knew? Learning this has been life-changing for me. Gentleness comes from wisdom, and the fear of God is the beginning of wisdom. (See Proverbs 9:10.) When we have a respectful fear of the Lord, we apply wisdom to our treatment of those made in His image. God's wisdom helps us as caregivers to conduct ourselves well even in the most trying circumstances. God's wisdom enables us to respond gently when demands are overwhelming or our loved one's words are harsh or unkind. God's wisdom enables us to demonstrate good behavior that points back to Him.

May the Lord grant us wisdom and understanding that produce good works and good behavior throughout our caregiving season. May His wisdom consistently enable us to treat others with remarkable gentleness. And may our good conduct point our loved one and those around us to Jesus.

A CAREGIVER'S PRAYER

Lord, I want to be wise and understanding. I want to demonstrate good conduct and actions done with gentleness, even when I'm overwhelmed and exhausted. Will You please fill me with wisdom so that my behavior honors and pleases You and points others toward You?

Enable me, through Your wisdom, to display remarkably gentle behavior during the duration of my caregiving season. May my responses and tone be kind, tender, and gentle. May Your wisdom enable me to conduct myself well and honor You. However harshly I may be treated, may You help me, by Your grace and wisdom, to respond wisely and in gentleness. In Jesus's name, amen.

THOUGHTS FOR TODAY

- ✦ God's wisdom produces good conduct and gentleness in particular.

- ✦ When I respectfully fear the Lord, I will wisely treat those made in His image with gentleness.

- ✦ God's wisdom enables me to respond gently when demands are overwhelming or my loved one's words are harsh or unkind.

MY THOUGHTS AND PRAYERS

_____

_____

_____

_____

_____

_____

DAY FORTY-NINE
KNOWING HIM MORE CHANGES EVERYTHING

He is my faithful love and my fortress, my stronghold and my
deliverer. He is my shield, and I take refuge in him.
—Psalm 144:2

When my life was upended through the new reality of caring for my infant granddaughter, knowing Christ personally and *intimately* by knowing His Word brought priceless comfort, reassurance, and peace to me during a frightening, chaotic time. Deep peace. Stabilizing peace. Isn't that what our hearts most yearn for when life goes topsy-turvy? We long for calming reassurance. We long to know that even in an uncertain season that we didn't anticipate or necessarily want, our hearts can find stability. And they can! Jesus is our Rock. (See 1 Corinthians 10:4.) He can be the primary stabilizing force in our lives.

Jesus is the Word of God. *"In the beginning was the Word, and the Word was with God, and the Word was God"* (John 1:1). *"The Word became flesh and dwelt among us"* (John 1:14). If Jesus is the Word made flesh, how can we possibly know Him apart from knowing Scripture? Do we read our Bibles? Listen to the Word, perhaps? Meditate on it? Do we write down verses that thrill our hearts so we can read them consistently? They may not be fancy or complicated, but these simple, essential practices cement God's truth firmly in our hearts and minds. And this makes all the difference.

Psalm 144:2 has guided, comforted, and strengthened me during my caregiving season, and it will do the same for you. Through this verse, I discovered that God is my *faithful love*. That term took my breath away. God is loyally committed to you and me, and His affections do not wander. I learned He is my fortress and my stronghold— the safe place I can run for protection and security. I can entrust my emotions, my heart, and all the circumstances of my life to Him, and so can you.

God is my deliverer. He frees my mind from inaccurate, sinful thoughts. He frees my heart from wounds and grief. He will also do this for you. He is my shield, stepping between me and the enemy's schemes and evil plans, and He is your shield, as well.

The degree to which we know Jesus—through Scripture—is the degree to which we will walk in peace. May He give you the desire and capacity to know Him more.

A CAREGIVER'S PRAYER

Dear Lord Jesus, I desire to know You more intimately and personally. Give me a deep and abiding love for You and Your Word. Thank You that as I make the time and effort to know You more through reading Your Word, listening to Your Word, and meditating on Your Word, I am filled with Your priceless comfort, reassurance, and deep, stabilizing peace.

As I continue to help my loved one, satisfy me with Your calming reassurance, especially in chaotic moments and on rough days. I'm grateful that You are my faithful love and my fortress, my stronghold and my deliverer. You are my shield, and I take refuge in You. In Your name, amen.

THOUGHTS FOR TODAY

+ If Jesus is the Word made flesh, how can I possibly know Him apart from knowing Scripture?

+ I can read my Bible, listen to it, write down verses to read repeatedly, and meditate on it.

+ The degree to which I know Jesus—through Scripture—is the degree to which I will walk in peace.

MY THOUGHTS AND PRAYERS

_____

_____

_____

_____

_____

_____

HIS LIGHT IS GREATER

Light shines in the darkness for the upright. He is gracious,
compassionate, and righteous.
—Psalm 112:4

I sat on the floor of our bedroom, gazing out at the snow sparkling on the ground in our backyard. Sunlight spilled through the windows, brightening the carpet and warming my upturned face. Every winter morning found me here, basking in golden rays while I could. Soon enough, the sun would head over the roof of our house, leaving the majority of our home shaded. So I took advantage and immersed myself in the sun each morning, knowing that long, dark winter afternoons and nights would ensue. Those mornings seated next to the window got me through wintertime.

There are times in caregiving that feel much like the cold shadows of winter. Our souls shiver as the darkness of doubt, fear, and discouragement plunges into our unsuspecting hearts. But if we are wise, we will bask in the light of God's truth while we can. John 12:35 advises us, *"Walk in the light while you can, so the darkness will not overtake you"* (NLT). The enemy of our souls works hard to oppose our best efforts. He wants to overtake us with his lies so that we are of no use to our loved one. Drawing close to God through reading His Word and prayer is the equivalent of sitting in front of a sunlit window on a winter day. The light of the Lord's truth encourages and lifts our weary hearts, enabling us to see exactly what's happening so we can resist the devil's evil schemes.

Oh, how our hearts greatly need the light of God's Word to strengthen us, uplift us, and encourage us through every wintery moment. When we're taken by surprise, when we're utterly overwhelmed, when our hearts sense discouragement encroaching, when dark thoughts bombard our minds, and when our hope is evaporating, today's verse reminds us, *"His light shines in the darkness for the upright."* We are the upright. We are God's dearly beloved children. (See Ephesians 5:1.)

Psalm 23:4 brings bright hope amid our darkness: *"Even when I go through the darkest valley, I fear no danger, for you are with me; your rod and your staff—they comfort me."* Despite the enemy's fiercest efforts, however dark the valley we walk through, God is with us.

The truth of God's spectacular light—the truth of His Word—shines into our hearts, bringing clarity, promise, and hope. We don't have to worry, we don't have to fear, because the Lord, who is gracious, compassionate, and righteous, is always with us. And His light is greater.

A CAREGIVER'S PRAYER

Lord, when my soul shivers as the wintry winds of doubt, fear, and discouragement blow, help me to bask in the light of Your spectacular truth. Encourage and lift my weary heart and grant me discernment to recognize what's happening so that, in Your grace and strength, I can resist the devil's evil schemes.

When I'm overwhelmed, when discouragement encroaches, when dark thoughts bombard my mind and my hope starts to evaporate, may Your truth and light strengthen and encourage me through every wintry moment. I praise You that Your light shines in the darkness for the upright, and that's me. I am Your beloved child, and I am grateful. In Jesus's name, amen.

THOUGHTS FOR TODAY

+ If I am wise, I will bask in the light of God's truth while I can.

+ My heart greatly needs the light of God's Word to strengthen, uplift, and encourage me through every wintry moment.

+ I don't have to worry or fear because the Lord, who is gracious, compassionate, and righteous, is always with me.

MY THOUGHTS AND PRAYERS

_____

_____

_____

_____

_____

_____

BE GLAD TODAY

This is the day the LORD has made;
let's rejoice and be glad in it.
—Psalm 118:24

"It's a beautiful day!" my precious granddaughter announces almost daily. She is always accurate. Her sweet, enthusiastic refrain makes me smile and reminds me to appreciate today (and I need reminding!). Whether sunny or cloudy, humid or dry, windy or calm, it is, in fact, the day God has made. We can recognize and appreciate it. Wherever the day finds us, and whatever the day holds, the psalmist encourages us to rejoice and be glad in it.

Is it always easy to rejoice? Umm, no. As caregivers, we most likely struggle with long to-do lists, as our loved one is either incapacitated in some way or far too old or young to manage without us. We also juggle our issues. Perhaps we're not sleeping well or have physical issues or discomforts. But in all our doing, in our managing, in our caring, and in spite of our legitimate concerns, we can ask the Lord for grace to rejoice and be glad anyway.

Praying for a glad heart is vital as we care for our loved one. Taking care of a small child while over the age of (ahem) sixty has been a challenging joy. My body reminds me that I'm no longer in my twenties. Though I stretch each morning, walk 2.5 miles nearly every day, and avoid processed foods, there's no denying reality.

Whatever our limitations, Proverbs 15:15 pretty much leaves us without excuse: *"He who has a glad heart has a continual feast [regardless of circumstances]"* (AMPC). Our hearts can be glad regardless of our circumstances. Our good heavenly Father, the giver of every good and perfect gift (see James 1:17), will make our hearts glad when we ask Him.

If we're busy rejoicing, we'll be far less likely to feel sorry for ourselves. This enables us to enjoy the day the Lord has made. Whatever is on the schedule, may the Lord enable each of us to remember that it really is a beautiful day—the one He has made. And may He give us grace to rejoice with a glad heart and be truly glad in it.

A CAREGIVER'S PRAYER

Lord, will You please give me the grace to appreciate each beautiful day You have made, and to rejoice and be glad in it, in spite of whatever personal issues I'm walking through? As I take care of my loved one, make my heart glad anyway. Grant me a cheerful heart that has a continuous feast—despite the circumstances.

Enable me to be so busy rejoicing, I won't feel sorry for myself. I lift up all the days on my upcoming caregiving schedule, and only You know the duration and outcome. I ask You to give me a glad heart and for the grace to be truly glad in the day You have made. In Jesus's name, amen.

THOUGHTS FOR TODAY

+ In all my doing, managing, and caring, and in spite of my concerns, I can ask the Lord for grace to rejoice and be glad.

+ I can ask the Lord to grant me a glad, cheerful heart.

+ If I'm busy rejoicing, I'll be far less likely to feel sorry for myself. This will help me to enjoy the day the Lord has made.

MY THOUGHTS AND PRAYERS

_____

_____

_____

_____

_____

_____

DAY FIFTY-TWO
LET HIS PEACE RULE

And let the peace of Christ, to which you were also called
in one body, rule your hearts.
—Colossians 3:15

When we are caregivers, the peace of Christ is not simply an option that we occasionally sprinkle into our lives like croutons and bacon bits at a salad bar. It's the meat and potatoes that fill our plates. But, just like standing in front of a succulent salad bar, we're in charge of what goes onto our plates. We must choose wisely. It's up to us to allow peace to rule in our hearts.

Paul says that we must *"let"* the peace of Christ rule our hearts. This means when stress hits hard or heaviness attempts to weigh us down, instead of making room on our plates for all that steals our peace, we can instead let the nourishing goodness of the meat of peace take up all the space. Letting Christ's peace reign means our hearts automatically say no to anything else. When His peace rules our hearts, we're not as vulnerable to life's hardships and the enemy's schemes, because there just isn't room for worry or stress or despair.

If Jesus is always with us (and He is—see Matthew 28:20), and we know Him intimately, we will be able to navigate the uncertainties and difficulties caregiving regularly presents with deep peace. Through the years that I have cared for our granddaughter, I can honestly say that I've been amazed at the difference His peace makes in my daily life. It's supernaturally stabilizing because Jesus is the Rock; He doesn't change and doesn't move. Knowing Him and His Word makes us stable, too. He is trustworthy. Jesus is the same yesterday, today, and forever. (See Hebrews 13:8.)

Jesus offers us meaningful peace—game-changing peace— because He is the Prince of Peace. (See Isaiah 9:6.) His dominion is peace, and when we allow Him full reign in our hearts, His supernatural peace takes over. Moves in. Ousts all else. When Christ's peace rules in our hearts, nothing can shake us. Not bad news. Not bad days. Not bad words or a bad diagnosis. Choose wisely. His peace can reign in our lives if we allow it.

A CAREGIVER'S PRAYER

Lord, help me to learn how to allow Your peace to rule in my heart. May Your supernatural peace so deeply and completely fill my heart that I'm not as vulnerable to life's hardships and the enemy's schemes. May I know that You are always with me, and may I know You intimately and therefore be able to navigate all the caregiving ups and downs with deep peace.

Jesus, You are my Rock. Please supernaturally stabilize me and enable me to live a life marked by peace. May Your peace consistently rule in my heart so that nothing can shake me. Help me to choose wisely by letting the peace of Christ rule in my heart. In Jesus's name, amen.

THOUGHTS FOR TODAY

+ We must choose wisely. It's up to us to allow peace to rule in our hearts.

+ Jesus offers us meaningful peace, game-changing peace, because He is the Prince of Peace.

+ When Christ's peace rules in our hearts, nothing can shake us.

MY THOUGHTS AND PRAYERS

_____

_____

_____

_____

_____

_____

DAY FIFTY-THREE
HE IS OUR HELP

God is our refuge and strength, a very present help in trouble.
—Psalm 46:1 ESV

What started as an ordinary morning rapidly escalated into a state of panic. After giving our then-infant granddaughter her bottle, I eased her onto my shoulder and began patting her back. She had recently started fussing and spitting up more, but this time was different. This time, she spat up blood. I nearly fainted.

Having just moved to a new state and with no pediatrician connections, my daughter and I immediately packed up and headed to a hospital about an hour away. Because of COVID-19, only one of us was allowed into the hospital with the baby—naturally, it was her deeply concerned mother who went, while I spent most of the day alternately pacing the sidewalk outside the hospital doors and texting my daughter for updates from the front seat of my car, feeling very much afraid and helpless. Though I couldn't be with my daughter and granddaughter inside the hospital, I could certainly pray. And, boy, did I ever.

Caregivers walk through many health issues with their loved one, some serious, others less so. One certainly feels frazzled and disconcerted when sudden health changes take place. How comforting and reassuring to know that God is a very present help in trouble. Oh, how our frantic hearts need Him. God is not distant but present. He is with us. He stands next to us and strengthens us (see 2 Timothy 4:17), so we can cope, think clearly, and function effectively. We can do whatever the situation demands.

In the midst of medical drama, heartache, and confusion, today's passage reminds us that God is our strength. Through Him we can stand and continue standing. Through His strength, we can offer encouragement and prayer to our loved one. When all around us is chaos, God is the refuge, the place of quiet calm and safety, to which we can run. God Himself is the secret place who offers our overwhelmed hearts shelter, courage, and peace.

It turns out that our granddaughter had severe reflux (which caused the bleeding) from infant formula that did not agree with her. After switching to a new formula, she made a complete recovery. As for me, through baby fevers, allergic reactions, toddler meltdowns, and all the childhood issues every parent (and grandparent) deals with, God remains my ever-present help. May He be yours, as well.

A CAREGIVER'S PRAYER

Lord, You know the various health issues I have helped my loved one through as a caregiver. When I am frazzled and disconcerted, may I remember that You, God, are a very present help in trouble. When their health plummets, may Your strength continually uphold me and enable me to cope, think clearly, and function.

Help me run to You, my refuge, when I am overwhelmed during frightening health situations. When chaos surrounds me, I will run to You, my refuge, my place of quiet calm and safety. Thank You for offering my sometimes-overwhelmed heart shelter, courage, and peace. Thank You for being my help. In Jesus's name, amen.

THOUGHTS FOR TODAY

+ I am comforted and reassured knowing that God is a very present help in trouble.

+ In fact, the Lord stands by me and strengthens me.

+ When all around me is chaos, God is the refuge, the place of quiet calm and safety to which I can run.

MY THOUGHTS AND PRAYERS

_____

_____

_____

_____

_____

_____

DAY FIFTY-FOUR
HE CARRIES OUR HEAVY LOAD

Blessed be the Lord! Day after day he bears our burdens.
—Psalm 68:19

Each weekday when I pick our granddaughter up from her K-4 preschool class, we walk out of her room and into the hallway, where her backpack hangs (among many) on a hook beneath her photo and name. She strolls right past her cute, heart-covered backpack because she knows Grammy will grab it. And Grammy does grab it because that cute backpack, loaded with her lunchbox, water bottle, extra change of clothes—and much more—is heavy. Very heavy.

It is sweet to me that my little granddaughter knows I will indeed grab her large, weighty backpack. It's not that she's unwilling to carry it, but she's extremely petite. What's difficult for her tiny frame is easy for me, and since, by the end of the school day, she is tired, I don't mind carrying it at all.

David, who wrote the psalm where today's verse is found, understood the benefits of a mighty God who would carry what David alone could never manage. *"Blessed be the Lord!"* he exclaimed, praising God for bearing his heavy burdens faithfully, day after day. David exuded awareness and gratitude that God bore his burdens daily.

And our faithful God does the same for us. As caregivers, we have burdens that are varied and numerous. We oversee laundry, hygiene, menus, medications, different appointments, and so much more. How encouraging to know that as we shoulder so many concerns, our faithful God helps lighten our load. He bears our burdens, knowing they are far too heavy for us to manage on our own. This includes emotional and mental burdens, even the ones no one else is aware of. He knows! *"Surely he has borne our griefs and carried our sorrows"* (Isaiah 53:4 ESV).

When we sag under the weight of all that is required of us in this season, we can rest in the loving presence of our good heavenly Father, who pours out His abundant grace and comes alongside us, lifting our "backpacks" crammed full of heavy sorrows and worries.

In His loving kindness, God does not expect us to be muscle-flexing super-people. He does expect us to know that He will help us and lighten our load. How good to know that it's not all up to us. We don't have to carry it all. Because of God's faithfulness, we can, like David, rejoice and say, "*Blessed be the Lord! Day after day he bears our burdens.*"

A CAREGIVER'S PRAYER

Lord, as I take care of my loved one, the burdens I carry are many and heavy. You are aware of how this affects me emotionally and mentally. And so, Lord, I lift each concern up to You, and with deep gratitude I thank You for carrying my burdens faithfully, day after day.

Thank You, Lord, that it's not all up to me. I don't have to carry it all because You help me. What is difficult for me is easy for You, and You lift the heavy load that I cannot manage alone. So, like David, I say, with immense gratitude, "Blessed be the Lord! Day after day he bears our burdens." In Jesus's name, amen.

THOUGHTS FOR TODAY

+ When I sag under the weight of all that is required of me, I can rest in the One who pours out His abundant grace and lifts my "backpack" full of heavy worries.

+ In His great faithfulness, God lifts even my mental and emotional burdens.

+ Because of God's faithfulness, I can, like David, rejoice and say, "*Blessed be the Lord! Day after day he bears our burdens.*"

MY THOUGHTS AND PRAYERS

_____

_____

_____

_____

_____

_____

_____

HELP FOR AN OVERWHELMED HEART

From the ends of the earth, I cry to you for help when my heart
is overwhelmed. Lead me to the towering rock of safety,
for you are my safe refuge,
a fortress where my enemies cannot reach me.
—Psalm 61:2–3 NLT

Though it wasn't the ends of the earth, it might as well have been. Just days after undergoing hip replacement surgery, my husband needed help getting dressed. So, in our oversized bedroom closet, I knelt beside him, attempting to wiggle his shorts over his uncooperative foot. As I did, tears dripped down my cheeks. Physically exhausted from caring for an almost-two-year-old full-time, I already had precious little margin in my days. Keith's at-home recovery, with all its demands on me, pushed my overwhelmed heart (and body) to the brink. I quietly wiped my tears, helped him to the recliner, and hurried back into the closet for a good cry. And I cried out to God for help.

Feelings of being totally overwhelmed snuck up on me that day. I think that often happens to caregivers. While we're in serving mode, sometimes, by necessity, our own needs move to the back burner—and they can surge to the forefront when we least expect it. That's why we need to pay attention. Listen to our hearts. And, like David, take time to process our emotions and struggles with the Lord when we are able.

The good news is that whether we're at the farthest corner of the earth or in our bedroom closet, our hearts don't have to remain overwhelmed; we can cry out to the Lord for help. How interesting to discover that David, who wrote this psalm, experienced these same feelings. And in classic David style, he plainly vented what he was currently walking through. Then, through his prayer, he asked for help and remembered where his answer—the remedy of his situation—exists.

Through David's beautiful prayer, we learn that God takes us from the ends of the earth (or our bedroom closet) to the One who can calm, comfort, and stabilize our weary, overwhelmed hearts. Jesus is our towering Rock of safety. He is the safe Refuge where we will find assurance, relief, and strength—the place where the enemies of discouragement and defeat can no longer influence us. When we go to Him, we'll find all that our overwhelmed hearts need.

A CAREGIVER PRAYER

Lord, thank You for enabling me to recognize when I am overwhelmed and for the reassurance of knowing that I can process all I am experiencing with You. As I cry out to You, thank You for encouraging and comforting me and for protecting me from discouragement, feelings of defeat, and any other of the enemy's attacks.

When I am on the brink of feeling overwhelmed, lead me to You, Jesus. You love me and care about all I'm walking through, and You are my Rock of safety. Give me a fresh perspective of You, Jesus, as my safe place of refuge. Thank You for calming, stabilizing, and strengthening me in this season. Help me to remember that my heart is safe and secure inside the fortress of Your unfailing love. In Your name, amen.

THOUGHTS FOR TODAY

+ I will listen to my heart and make time to process my emotions with the Lord.

+ As I pray and ask, Jesus protects me from discouragement and defeat.

+ Jesus hears my cries, and He will strengthen, calm, and help me.

MY THOUGHTS AND PRAYERS

_____

_____

_____

_____

_____

_____

DAY FIFTY-SIX
OUR LIVING HOPE

Blessed be the God and Father of our Lord Jesus Christ!
According to his great mercy,
he has caused us to be born again to a living hope through the
resurrection of Jesus Christ from the dead.
—1 Peter 1:3 ESV

How's your hope holding up? It can be tricky to maintain hope throughout our caregiving journey for assorted reasons. One is that we don't necessarily know the outcome. This in itself can be agonizing and a matter of ongoing, fervent prayer. Neither do we necessarily know how long we will be caring for our loved one. Again, it's hard because living life on hold isn't easy or convenient. And sometimes just our daily caregiving routine—the ongoing difficulties, pressures, and struggles—feels endless and overwhelming. There are times we can almost feel the hope draining right out of our pores.

As believers, however, we know that our hope is not to be hitched to our circumstances. Our hope stands alone, and His name is Jesus. When we are born again, this living hope—Christ Himself—rushes inside our hearts and makes His abode there. He has caused each one of us to be born again to a living hope. This means that our hope is not dormant. It isn't expired. It is a living, thriving hope because it exists in the very alive, triumphant person of Jesus Christ, who imparts this priceless hope into our hearts.

When we're immersed in the difficult waters of day-to-day care for our loved one, because we are rooted in Christ, we continue to stand in hope, despite the struggles. Our circumstances do not determine our hope; our Savior does. As we grow in Christ, securing our hearts in the truth of His Word, we are *"being rooted and built up in him and established in the faith"* (Colossians 2:7). And we're also being rooted and built up and established in hope.

I find it wind-blowing-in-my-hair liberating to hitch my hope firmly to my Jesus. On good days, on bad days, on "you've got to be kidding me" days, we can still have hope because we still have our Savior. When crazy circumstances drag our hearts up, down, and all around, our hope can still flourish because Jesus is the same, yesterday, today, and forever. He is our dependable, awesome, mighty, living hope.

A CAREGIVER'S PRAYER

Lord, although I don't know the outcome of my caregiving situation or exactly how long I will be serving in this capacity, I don't want to lose hope. Help me not to hitch my hope to my circumstances but to Jesus, who is my living hope. May this living, thriving hope fill me just as Christ Himself fills my heart.

On days when I struggle most, help me to continue standing in Christ, rooted in Him. I'm grateful that I can still flourish because Jesus is the same, yesterday, today, and forever. He is my dependable, awesome, mighty, living hope. May my hope continue to thrive and flourish because it is hitched to the very alive, triumphant person of Jesus Christ. It's in His name that I pray, amen.

THOUGHTS FOR TODAY

+ As a believer, my hope is not to be hitched to my circumstances but to Jesus.

+ Because I am rooted in Christ, I can continue to stand in hope, in spite of struggles.

+ On good days, bad days, and "you've got to be kidding me" days, Jesus is my dependable, awesome, mighty, and living hope.

MY THOUGHTS AND PRAYERS

_____

_____

_____

_____

_____

_____

DAY FIFTY-SEVEN
FLING EVERY CARE

Casting the whole of your care [all your anxieties,
all your worries, all your concerns, once and for all] on Him,
for He cares for you affectionately and
cares about you watchfully.
—1 Peter 5:7 AMPC

Band-Aids are a precious commodity around my house. Not because my husband and I constantly fall and scrape our knees or cut our fingers while chopping the lettuce, but because our magnifying-glass-using granddaughter can spot the tiniest, slightest, nearly invisible blemish on her pristine skin and then adamantly declare that she absolutely must be bandaged. Immediately. While I appreciate her thoroughness, most of the time, no actual bandage is required. But I'm glad she comes to me, because when I stoop down and say, "Let me see," she knows that I genuinely listen and care.

Just as I always bend down to examine her (real or imagined) boo-boos, God likewise tenderly watches over us and all of the matters that concern us. Today's verse emphasizes that the Lord cares for us affectionately and watchfully. Like a parent tenderly watching over their child, God keeps a watchful eye on us because He loves us.

The apostle Peter knew the secret of thriving in ministry and under intense persecution. He understood the value of sharing every struggle, every worry, every iota—*all of it* that concerned him and created anxiety in his heart—with the One who tenderly watched over his soul. As caregivers, we would benefit from following his lead. Peter regularly handed his anxieties to God through prayer. He sat and walked with the Lord, pointing out and sharing all of his worries.

When we struggle under soul-crushing worries of our own, God, who affectionately and watchfully cares for us, is always available. It doesn't matter if what we're bringing to the Lord is massive or minuscule. We don't have to walk around with wounds and sores in need of bandaging. When we're anxious, dealing with disappointment, and struggling with fear or exhaustion, it's such a wholesome, healthy relief to share it all with the One who truly cares. The Lord understands the season we're in and the burdens we carry. He loves us with an everlasting love. Whether our hearts require bandaging or not, our good heavenly Father stoops down and says, "Let Me see." So, go ahead and fling every care straight into His everlasting arms.

A CAREGIVER'S PRAYER

Lord, thank You for loving me, watching over me affectionately, and caring for me watchfully. My goal from this point forward is to share with You every struggle, every worry, every iota of all that concerns me and causes anxiety in my heart. Thank You for stooping down to listen.

Father, thank You for always making Yourself available to me. Whether the matter I bring to You is massive or minuscule, I'm grateful that I don't have to pretend it's not there and that You will take it from me and bandage it if necessary. Thank You for loving me so well. In Jesus's name, amen.

THOUGHTS FOR TODAY

- ✦ Like a parent tenderly watching over their child, God keeps watch over me because He loves me.
- ✦ When I struggle under soul-crushing worries, God, who affectionately and watchfully cares for me, is always available.
- ✦ The Lord cares for me affectionately and watchfully.

MY THOUGHTS AND PRAYERS

_____

_____

_____

_____

_____

_____

DAY FIFTY-EIGHT
ETERNAL PERSPECTIVE

For we do not have an enduring city here; instead,
we seek the one to come.
—Hebrews 13:14

Several years ago, while visiting my sister and her family in my home state of Michigan, we decided to drive into Detroit—the city where we had once lived and where our grandparents and great-grandparents had lived before us. Way back then, it was safe for me to walk home from school by myself, even as a first grader. Sometimes I would call my Gram and make arrangements to walk several blocks to her house after school instead.

Oh, how I loved my Gram and her cozy little house. It was always clean. She always cooked delicious homemade meals. Best of all, there were plenty of cookies in her big Tupperware container, and her backyard included an above-ground pool.

During this visit several years ago, my sister and I eagerly turned onto the street where our grandparents had lived, eager to see their house and bask in nostalgic memories. But as our car approached their address, our hearts sank. The house was gone. All that remained was a vacant lot with a few scattered piles of trash. That area of the city had fallen into disrepair and dilapidation. Tears of disappointment stung my eyes. Thankfully, vivid memories remain tucked in my heart.

Today's verse of Scripture offers much-needed perspective. Everything on earth is in the process of decaying. Our bodies are decaying. (See 2 Corinthians 4:16.) The address where we currently serve as caregivers may not always be there. The lovely, tree-lined streets of our youth may no longer exist. But *"there is a river whose streams make glad the city of God"* (Psalm 46:4 esv).

As we take care of our loved one, how important it is to hold the eternal perspective that the place(s) on earth where our life unfolds is not all there is. The village, town, or city where we now live will not endlessly endure. Consider ancient Rome. What was once a thriving metropolis and the most powerful nation on earth is now a tourist town of ruins. But, if we allow it, each of these realities points us toward the enduring city to come—the eternal city, which *"has no need of sun or moon to shine on it, for the glory of God gives it light, and its lamp is the Lamb"* (Revelation 21:23 ESV).

May the Lord, who enables us to serve Him through serving our precious loved one, grant us the eternal perspective our hearts desperately yearn for. And may we remember that although we do not have an enduring city here, we can instead seek the one to come.

A CAREGIVER'S PRAYER

Lord, thank You for helping me understand that everything on earth is in a state of decay. Help me maintain the accurate perspective that where I currently live and the place where I currently serve as a caregiver are not all there is. May these realities point me toward the enduring city that is to come, the eternal city, where "the glory of God gives it light, and its lamp is the Lamb."

As I serve my precious loved one, by Your great grace, grant me the eternal perspective my heart desperately yearns for. Help me to remember that although I do not have an enduring city here, I can instead seek the one to come. In Jesus's name, amen.

THOUGHTS FOR TODAY

+ Everything on earth is in the process of decaying.

+ As I take care of my loved one, it's vital that I hold the eternal perspective that the place(s) on earth where my life unfolds is not all there is.

+ May I remember that although I do not have an enduring city here, I can instead seek the one to come.

MY THOUGHTS AND PRAYERS

_____

_____

_____

_____

_____

_____

DAY FIFTY-NINE
FINISH THE COURSE

But I consider my life of no value to myself; my purpose is to
finish my course and the ministry I received from the Lord
Jesus, to testify to the gospel of God's grace.
—Acts 20:24

I'm convinced that the caregiving work we're currently involved in was appointed to each of us by the Lord Jesus. It is a sacred assignment, and my prayer for each of us is that we will complete this vital ministry with excellence. This means we won't quit. We won't waffle in our commitment. It means that in comparison to our lives, the divine purpose of this assignment holds more value than our very lives, as the apostle Paul says above.

As we minister to our loved one—and make no mistake, this is indeed a sacred ministry—our actions testify to the gospel of God's grace. It is through His grace alone that we persevere on hard days. It is through His grace alone that we endure and keep showing up. And this effusive grace will be evident to our loved one and to those around us. God's grace working in us and through us actually testifies to the gospel of God's grace. How remarkable is it that as we quietly, faithfully, and obediently do the work entrusted to us, God's grace is on full display, and He is ultimately glorified.

Knowing all this enables us to reject the temptations that the enemy loves to flash before our faces. It means we can be strong and not succumb to self-pity. It means we will not yield to exasperation. It means that we refuse to give in to confusion or despair. Because we understand and accept our current purpose, we will *"be strong in the Lord [be empowered through your union with Him]; draw your strength from Him [that strength which His boundless might provides]"* (Ephesians 6:10 AMPC).

God's boundless might enables us to serve to a degree and length we could never accomplish otherwise. His strength is the backbone that holds us up, solidifying our commitment. Our union with Christ empowers us to persevere with strength. Remaining close to Him through it all, drawing our strength from Him, is how we finish the course, and finish it well.

A CAREGIVER'S PRAYER

Lord, I believe that the caregiving work I am currently involved in was appointed to me by You and that it is a sacred ministry. Help me not to quit or waver in my commitment but to finish my course well, glorifying You.

Enable me to reject the temptations of self-pity, exasperation, confusion, despair, and any other lie that the enemy flashes before my face. Help me to be strong in You, Lord, and in the power of Your might. Give me great grace to quietly, faithfully, and obediently do the work You have entrusted to me. As I do, may Your grace be on full display to those around me, and may You be glorified. In Jesus's name, amen.

THOUGHTS FOR TODAY

+ The caregiving work I am currently involved in was appointed to me by the Lord Jesus.

+ It is a sacred ministry.

+ As I quietly, faithfully, and obediently do the work entrusted to me, God's grace is on full display, and He is ultimately glorified.

MY THOUGHTS AND PRAYERS

_____

_____

_____

_____

_____

_____

DAY SIXTY
FINISH THE RACE AND KEEP THE FAITH

I have fought the good fight, I have finished the race,
I have kept the faith.
—2 Timothy 4:7

Our time together is coming to an end, and I want you to know that, although we probably have not met, I have held you close in my heart while writing and have prayed for you. I cannot help but sense a kindred spirit between us because we're on similar journeys. I actually feel sentimental about our time together. Every word has been written by God's grace, with you in mind, specifically aimed at your heart. I pray that He has used and will continue to use His Word and this book to bless, equip, and strengthen you as you care for your loved one.

I don't know where you are on your caregiving journey. Perhaps you are just getting started. Maybe you've been at it for several years. But I do know that, like me, you have probably been taxed and stretched and strained beyond what you ever imagined. This is a good thing because it means God is training us, stretching us, and growing our faith. He is teaching us to rely on Him more deeply.

In today's Scripture, we read one of Paul's most famous statements. It was not written boastfully but with acute awareness that his own time on earth was coming to a close. He was able to declare, "*I have fought the good fight, I have finished the race, I have kept the faith*," because he knew, deep down, that by God's grace he had accomplished all that was required of him on this earth. He had not grown weary in well-doing. He had endured. He has pressed on "*to reach the end of the race and receive the heavenly prize for which God, through Christ Jesus, is calling us*" (Philippians 3:14 NLT).

This is my fervent prayer for each of us as caregivers: that we will, by God's effusive grace at work in us, press on, fight the good fight, finish the race, keep the faith, and receive the heavenly prize.

As Paul tells us in the verse which follows today's passage, *"There is reserved for me the crown of righteousness, which the Lord, the righteous Judge, will give me on that day, and not only to me, but to all those who have loved his appearing"* (2 Timothy 4:8).

And so, my caregiver friend, I entrust you and your journey to the One who is faithful. He has reserved for you the crown of righteousness, and I trust that you will one day hear, *"Well done, good and faithful servant! You were faithful over a few things; I will put you in charge of many things. Share your master's joy"* (Matthew 25:23).

I leave you with these final words of encouragement, from my heart to yours: *"Therefore, my dear brothers and sisters, be steadfast, immovable, always excelling in the Lord's work, because you know that your labor in the Lord is not in vain"* (1 Corinthians 15:58).

A CAREGIVER'S PRAYER

Lord, this season of caregiving has taxed, stretched, and strained me beyond what I ever imagined. And yet Your grace has always been there, sufficient for each task. As I care for my loved one, give me great grace to endure, to persevere, to fight the good fight, to finish the race, to keep the faith, and to receive the heavenly prize.

Help me to honor You by honoring this sacred commitment and doing it to the best of my ability. My longing is to hear Your words proclaiming over me, "Well done, good and faithful servant." Help me, Lord, to be steadfast, immovable, always excelling in the Lord's work, because I know that my labor in the Lord is not in vain. In Jesus's name, amen.

THOUGHTS FOR TODAY

- I will, by God's effusive grace at work in me, press on, fight the good fight, finish the race, keep the faith, and receive the heavenly prize.

+ "There is reserved for me the crown of righteousness, which the Lord, the righteous Judge, will give me on that day, and not only to me, but to all those who have loved his appearing" (2 Timothy 4:8).

+ I will be steadfast, immovable, always excelling in the Lord's work, because I know that my labor in the Lord is not in vain.

MY THOUGHTS AND PRAYERS

_____

_____

_____

_____

_____

_____

ABOUT THE AUTHOR

Julie K. Gillies is the author of *Prayers to Calm Your Anxious Heart: 100 Reassuring Devotions*; *From Hot Mess to Blessed*; and the devotional *Prayers for a Woman's Soul*. Her books, website, and YouTube channel help readers develop a love for and understanding of Scripture and encourage people to pray about everything to the One who always hears.

Julie is the joyful wife of Keith, mom of three adults, and Grammy of five. She currently serves as a caregiver for their youngest granddaughter while her mama works. She enjoys long walks in nature, baking from scratch, and any day without humidity.